DESIGNING STAGE COSTUMES

A PRACTICAL GUIDE

DESIGNING STAGE COSTUMES

A Practical Guide

Gary Thorne

The Crowood Press

First published in 2001 by
The Crowood Press Ltd
Ramsbury, Marlborough
Wiltshire SN8 2HR

© Gary Thorne 2001

British Library Cataloguing-in-Publication Data
A catalogue record for this book is available from the British Library.

ISBN 1 86126 416 X

Front cover credit: Ted Pearson as Pomponia in *Knight of the Burning Pestle.* Directors: Bernard Hopkins and Pat Galloway. Lighting: Kevin Fraser, Stratford Festival Theatre. Photography courtesy of the Stratford Festival Archives.

Back cover credit: Robert Bockstael playing Zastrozzi, Alberta Theatre Projects, Canada. Director: Bob White. Lighting: Harry Frehner. Photo: Trudie Lee.

Designed and edited by Focus Publishing, The Courtyard, 26 London Road, Sevenoaks, Kent TN13 1AP

Printed and bound in Great Britain by J.W. Arrowsmith, Bristol

Dedication
This book is with special dedication to my parents, family and friends, and especially Charles Russell.

Acknowledgements
Thank you to all the companies and individuals who have worked on the productions photographed within.

Designers: Margaret Harris of Motley, Alison Chitty, Tanya Moiseiwitsch, Ann Curtis, Desmond Heeley, Debra Hanson, Lewis Brown, Brian Jackson and Vikie Le Sache.

Theatre companies: Colchester Mercury Theatre, Pop Up Theatre, Polka Theatre, Unicorn Theatre, Forest Forge Theatre, Lyric Theatre, Guildhall School of Music and Drama, Art Educational Performing School, Royal Academy of Dramatic Art, Alberta Theatre Projects, Stratford Festival Theatre, London Grand Theatre and Mikado Bordeaux.

Directors: William Gaskill, Vicky Ireland, Roman Stefanski, Thomas de Mallet Burgess, Michael Miller, Michael Dalton, Penny Bernand, Jane Wolfson, Jonathan Holloway, David Robson, Adrian James, John Perry, Ian Goode, Ian Smith, Robert Howie, D. Micheal Dobbin, Bob White, David Latham. Michael Winter, Bernard Hopkins, David William, John Neville, Martha Henry, Derek Goldby, James Tillett and Karl Hibbert.

Photographers: Trudie Lee, Stratford Festival Archives, Roger Howard and Simon Annand.

Students at: Dali-Central St. Martins, Motley Theatre Design and the Royal Academy of Dramatic Art, Rose Bruford.

Special thanks to Neil Fraser at RADA, William Gaskill, Bryan Lewin, Charles P. Russell, Martha Henry and Teddy Atienza.

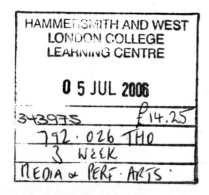

CONTENTS

A historical staging made more accessible and enjoyable through heightening the play's parody through exaggeration and cross casting. Andrew Akman as Mistress Merrythought and Juan Chioran as old Merrythought, Knight of the Burning Pestle, *Stratford Festival. Directors: Bernard Hopkins, Pat Galloway. Lighting: Kevin Fraser. Courtesy of the Stratford Festival Archives*

FOREWORD

by William Gaskill

You can do a play without a set but you can't do it without the costumes. Well, you can, but the audience would feel deeply cheated. I once saw an excellent fringe group in a version of the Arabian Nights but the poor actors were in practice clothes. It didn't work. Something essential in my expectation of theatre had been thwarted.

Our images of the great theatres of the past – the amphitheatres of Greece and Rome, the bare platform of Shakespeare's Globe – are of an actor in the space wearing something that sets him apart: masks and platform shoes, plumes in the hair, something that establishes him in the space and commands the audience's attention. With the coming of realism and the detailed presentation of contemporary life the function of costumes became equally important in defining the social existence of the characters and their precise psychology. But even in the most naturalist plays there must be a sense of the theatrical, of something that focuses the audience on the life of the character and the play.

What this is will change with the centuries. Garrick played Macbeth in knee breeches and a powered wig that would be laughable today. Some of today's costumes for Shakespeare are already laughable. To design clothes for the actor the designer has to have not only an awareness of the play but a keen sense of how to communicate this to a contemporary audience. Above all, the actor is dependent on the designer to feel right in the part, in the play and for the audience who will see it. This rightness is the designer's job.

Gary Thorne was lucky enough to be trained by Margaret Harris at the Motley Theatre Design Course. Margaret Harris designed John Gielgud's first production and during her long career she saw and led many of the changes in theatre design. She was able to pass on to Gary Thorne (and to many others) her own particular sense of theatre: pragmatic, practical, non-decorative, always responsive to the play and aware of the actor's needs, which he captures so well in this book.

INTRODUCTION

Set and costume design for the theatre is an engaging and rewarding experience. Whether it is for intimate, small-scale productions on tour, or for the vast space of an opera house, the experience will prove to be both creative and challenging. Space and budget constraints can lead to creative problem solving. Often, the smaller the performance space and the tighter the budget, the more innovative and ingenious the results will be. Production standards can be remarkably high in the school hall, community centre, amateur theatre and on the fringe. It only takes an enthusiastic team with a strong sense of determination and vision to deliver quality performance. The spark for ideas comes from within the play itself and the first read through of any play will prove an exciting experience.

The function of all theatre design is to support the play and its players. As with all forms of design there is a process, which will naturally involve trial and error, success and failure. New ideas rarely develop with ease and live performance will always involve taking risks, some of which may end in disaster.

To achieve success, the design process needs to be structured, involving effective administration and management, and the setting of parameters. Communication and collaboration with a wide range of talented individuals not only makes the experience particularly rewarding but is essential to the achievement of successful results.

It is very important that the character of the play is fully respected when designing costume. The playwright's intention steers design through its process. The costume needs to serve the play, and support the actor. It is a process of engagement through involvement. The act of creating the costume demands the use of both practical and imaginative skills. The process of getting a

Small-scale touring set, with accompanying designed seating. Pop in a Box.
Director: Penny Bernand. Pop-Up Theatre

Oliver performed by young people for a sophisticated theatre-going audience.
Director and setting: Jeremy James Taylor. Costumes: Sheila Darlington.
Bonnets: Alix Stone. National Youth Music Theatre

The young audience takes a close look at the
performance. Cast of Pop in a Box.
Costumes: Moe Casey

play 'on its feet' is full of obstacles and barriers, challenges and revelations, compromises and innovations.

The chief aim of this book is to enable the reader to participate in part of this process and to initiate a sense of enquiry, along with a spirit of adventure. Borrow plays from the library while working through the book and set yourself up with an act or scene to design. The issues raised will seem so much more real when a play is at hand.

Each chapter contains a range of exercises which will help to provide practical approaches to problem solving. One of the most common problems is an inability to provide adequate visual representation of what you are feeling. If this is your problem, just remember that once you begin drawing it gets easier with each day's practice. Draw regularly and make studies of people, objects and places.

Students at a drama school performing
Anatol. *Arts Educational.*
Director: Robert Freed. Lighting: Di Steadman

The opportunity for research is never ending and deeply fascinating. Surround yourself with books on art and design, performance, architecture, furniture, nature, human anatomy, photography, people and place. Everything is of interest – keep an open mind and develop an interest in the unusual. Visit galleries and museums, both locally and wherever you travel. Explore and inquire into all aspects of art and design, take full advantage of every opportunity for study and research, and you will thoroughly enjoy the process of creating costuming for the stage.

Local drama groups and amateur operatic societies often provide an opportunity to get involved. Community education centres offer part-time drama and design courses throughout the year, and regularly celebrate term ends with staged productions. Festivals and carnivals offer performance in the open air – costume and scenery on floats or in streets and parks, provide challenging creative opportunities. Behind the scenes are countless enthusiasts each with their individual speciality, each interested in celebration through collaboration.

Note: Students of theatre design have varied interests, skills and experiences. On a post-graduate level, student specialities may include fine art, design, architecture, interior design, engineering, craft, history, literature, performance, textiles and fashion.

INTRODUCTION TO MARTHA HENRY

Dispersed throughout this book, are a selection of quotes by the actress and director Martha Henry. The excerpts are the result of an interview. Each quote is placed alongside particular sections of the text with the aim of providing an insight to the reader on the significance of costume design for both the actor and director.

Martha Henry joined Canada's Stratford Festival Theatre in 1962. To date, she has performed over forty roles on the Stratford stage and is internationally recognized and respected as both an actress and a director, having worked in theatre, film and television in Canada, the USA and the UK. Martha Henry is the winner of five Best Actress Genie Awards and three Gemini Awards.

Costumes with small properties including briefcase, suitcase, toasting fork, air freshener, carpet cleaner and cane. Entertaining Mr Sloane. *Stratford Festival Theatre*

Characters drawn up as eccentric and comic to suit the musical style of commedia dell' arte types. Mascarde, Mikado, Bordeaux.

A basic costume with two looks. One more peasant-like, the other dressed up for the wedding. Starlight Cloak, Polka Theatre

1 DRESS SENSE AND THE INDIVIDUAL

CULTURAL INFLUENCES

How wide-ranging are your 'looks' and what purpose does each look serve? Must you adopt a certain appearance for work? Do you dress differently at home? How does event and occasion affect what you wear? What would you not be seen in while out socializing with friends? What are the major influences in how you dress?

The answers to these and similar questions reveal that individual dress choice is largely shaped by circumstance and situation. Location can also play a part. When we move considerable distances, climate may be the first influence, but differences in social values makes for more change. What seemed appropriate to wear in one place may seem entirely out of place in another.

Although anti-fashion trends are common, this is usually a reaction to the political, social or economic issues of the time. Anti-fashion images frequently have an ideological basis. Recent examples include the National Front, punks and skinheads. Other groups of people reject contémporary style and prefer to dress exclusively in clothes of another era. However, this is often as much an outward manifestation of a desire to escape the present through finding a spiritual haven in the past as an anti-fashion statement *per se*.

For the majority, however, the way in which we present ourselves to the world around us is heavily influenced by cultural constraints. Friends and colleagues affect the way we dress, particularly those we admire or aspire to know better. Affiliations, clubs, fraternities – all have their specified dress codes. We belong to these through blood, education, money, or membership, and thereby welcome their imposed identifiable 'look'. A golf club, for

A professional's working uniform which is stereotypically recognizable. The medical consultant. Reckless.
Alberta Theatre Projects

The editorial office printers.
Enemy of the People. *Stratford Festival Theatre*

example, may have a distinct dress code. Whilst some aspects of the clothing could be considered purely practical, the dress code reflects a recognizable and meaningful image which the members would acknowledge symbolizes their position in sporting society.

Think of the fraternities, affiliations and clubs that thrive in your community and consider their various dress codes. How involved is the membership and who might be excluded?

Members of various professions, trades and guilds may also adopt distinctive dress, the silhouette of which is easily recognized. A uniform has the same eye-catching properties.

All uniformity in dress, whether formal or casual, is a powerful symbol of membership – of belonging.

Exercise
Collect images that correspond to and reflect the differences of dress between friends and family. Observe them at work and at leisure. Note the cut of the garment and fabric type, paying attention to the different seasons. Variations in shaping can be seen in the suit – certain businesses show a preference for a specific cut and tailoring. There may also be established limits to skirt length or style of blouse. Cut and paste the results of your research into a sketchbook or scrapbook. Date the entry, noting name and age, occupation and interests. Flesh out the characters to clearly demonstrate what kind of individuals they are.

COMFORT

How often do you feel really comfortable in what you wear? Does the feel of fabric matter when making a purchase? Which fabrics cause you to itch, sweat, or suffer the cold? How do you feel when wearing similar styles of different fabric content? How does the cut and tailoring affect how you feel? Consider the characteristics that make a garment what it seems to be when worn.

Exercise
Make a list of all the garments in your wardrobe, including underwear, socks and nightwear. If your clothes are seasonal, make a separate list for each.

Example:
Garment: tailored suit, two-piece.
Date of purchase: 1998.
Garment use: office.
Fabric content, colour and texture: fine

A costume and small props drawing which helps enlighten the viewer on character interests.
Reckless. *Alberta Theatre Projects*

Scottish wool, with herringbone pattern. Feels smooth, warm, and of medium thickness. Smells natural. Dark blue-grey colour. The lining is a very smooth acetate, makes for comfortable movements.

Cleaning instructions: dry clean only.

Grade of comfort: formal – feels smart, makes me appear well dressed.

Character: mostly worn on more formal occasions, fine finish to the tailoring, warm on a cool winter's day.

Also include details of where each garment was purchased, how much it cost and what other articles it goes well with. It is often helpful to include a photograph of you wearing the garments.

OUTWARD APPEARANCE

Does the way you look affect the way people treat you? How important are the expectations of friends, family and colleagues at work to you? Do people make remarks about how you look? Do these comments initiate a turn further towards more individual expression? Have you ever been at a disadvantage because of what you wore? How and when do you feel inappropriately dressed? What impression do you like to give of yourself? Do you think this is how others see you?

FIT

Are you a lucky enough to be a standard size or are the majority of clothes uncomplimentary to your shape? Do you buy particular labels because of the fit? Do you like a snug fit for some occasions and a baggy one for others? How does the cut, drape, and fit of clothing affect your sense of ease and confidence? When sleeve cuffs or skirt hems are too short, trousers too tight in the hip and crotch, or when underwear rides up, how do you feel? When socks work their way down whilst walking, or the shirt pulls tight across the back shoulder blades, or when the neck is a bit on the tight side, what habits or manners do you adopt to counter it?

Begin looking around you and observe the habits and mannerisms which people adopt because of fit. Note what they are wearing and collect images depicting people at odds with their clothing.

ALLURE

How does romantic attraction manifest itself through dress? What makes you feel sexy, and what attracts you to others? Which of your garments draw the most admiring glances? History is rich in examples of dress accentuating the contours of the body. This shaping and what it reveals relates to sexual allure. Historical dress has been used to exaggerate, to draw attention to sexual characteristics. Are there relationships you can make between the articles you own and historical dress with respect to allure? Does the material itself attract the eye? Is it to do with the cut of the fabric? Does the fit of a romantically alluring costume suggest sexual awareness? When you wish to look romantically attractive, how careful are you with what you choose to wear?

How does hair have allure? Does its style, length, and colour suggest virility? What facial hair is alluring? How are wigs a sign of hygiene? What sexual characteristics are at play with styles and types of hair and wig? Can you style your hair differently, and what changes do you make for different occasions?

COLOUR

Which colours in your wardrobe would you consider the most sophisticated? What colour might be most alluring? Do those clothes which reveal or expose more of the body have an additional sexual characteristic through colour? Which colours do you tend to wear when you wish people to take you most seriously? What signals do the colours in your wardrobe send out?

The 'Real Me'

Which garments carry the stamp of 'you'? How much of this image is a part of the circle in which you move? How has this image changed over the past five and ten years? Put together a photo album of how you have changed over the years. Note what you were doing in and around the time of the photograph. Mention what the outfit you were wearing was intended for. Looking back on things, what would you have preferred to have been wearing? Consider the other fashions of the time. What kept you from dressing in another way?

Lifestyles

How often have you whispered 'If only I dared wear that'. Which clothes and what types of fabric catch your eye and excite your imagination? Would these outfits relate to specific activities? What lifestyles do you

Edward Atienza as Kemp showing him in a relaxed 'at home' manner. Entertaining Mr Sloane. *Stratford Festival Theatre*

Edward Atienza as Kemp, having just returned from the shops. Entertaining Mr Sloane. *Stratford Festival Theatre*

associate with them? How important is the fabric, cut, fit, colour and texture? Collect visual records of lifestyles and think about which appears to be the most 'alternative'. Find associations with music, art and design, food and drink, place and atmosphere, which link these people to their lifestyles.

Exercise
Create a list accompanied by images that suggests who you are. Note down:

- Physical stature in basic measurements, from head to toe.

Lifestyles suggested through a collage of mesh, tattoos, suspenders, fishnet tights, red vinyl boots, chain jewellery and stylized make-up. Collage for The Rocky Horror Show

- Posture when standing, sitting and relaxing.
- Complexion, colouring, hair and eye colour.
- Ethnic and cultural or ancestral background.
- Social life at work and home.
- Interests and hobbies.
- Home life, both present and past.
- Family influences, upbringing, education, qualifications and experiences.
- How seriously you treat both your work and leisure-time activities.
- Religion and beliefs, prejudices, fears, superstitions, taboos.
- Sense of direction.
- Idiosyncrasies and behaviour traits.
- Dislikes and anxieties.
- Fondest memories, happiest times.
- Most moving and sad occasions.
- Which animal and vegetable you see yourself as.
- Which people you see yourself like.
- How you like to dress.
- How you hate to dress.
- Any recurring fantasies concerning dress.
- Favourite colours and patterns, fabrics and styles.
- Politics and views on society and community.
- What you like to read, and favourite films and plays.
- How you prefer to spend time, whom you like to see the most.
- Places you love to visit, how you prefer to travel, where you prefer to stay and eat.
- Routines and disciplines in your daily, weekly and yearly schedule.
- The dreams you have for the things you most desire.

RADICAL CHANGE

What are the influences that create radical change in fashion? Have you seen such change?

17

A suggested threatening image, through a shaved head, studded leather and suede clothing, heavy biker boots and weaponry. Zastrozzi. *Alberta Theatre Projects*

What are the contributing factors? What is eccentric dress? What extraordinary people live in your society, who appear to dress as eccentrics? What dividing lines are drawn up by society that should not be overstepped? What is too anarchic?

Start a scrapbook collection of eccentric and radical looks, those that shock. Note the type of lifestyle associated with it, What reasons lie behind decisions to call or label something out of place? What leads society to state that some manners and codes of behaviour are unacceptable, wholly inappropriate, threatening or dangerous?

2 THEATRE MANAGEMENT AND THE PRODUCTION TEAM

Putting a play on to the stage involves teamwork. In order for a production to succeed, all those involved must collaborate and share responsibilities in addition to their individual functions.

The theatre administrator, artistic director, production manager and technical director prepare the way forward for production. This, in many cases, is long before a play or plays are chosen. The pre-production period can involve weeks, months or years of planning and decision making.

Establishing the performing venue and choosing a play often goes in hand with choosing the director and design team. This team will comprise designers for set, costume, lighting, sound, and music. The choreo–grapher and fight director may also collaborate closely with the director and design team at the initial stages of planning.

An early presentation, made to the production department heads and stage management by the director and design team, informs the management staff of the workload, and it is often at this time that a team of makers and construction staff are contracted.

The production period often begins well in advance of rehearsal. Actors will have been contracted by this time, along with the appropriate numbers of backstage or crew members. By the time the rehearsal period commences, a considerable amount of production work will probably have been achieved.

FUNCTIONS OF THEATRE MANAGEMENT AND PRODUCTION STAFF

Administrator and General Manager
- Administers and manages a theatre or company and its financing.
- Obtains permission to perform plays and music, negotiates royalty fees.
- Obtains licences and certificates for health and safety.
- Defines production budgets and contracts for staff, directors, designers and cast.
- Establishes the box office and arranges publicity.
- Prepares and announces auditions.

The Artistic Director
- Defines the artistic vision by selecting plays.
- Establishes an artistic standard.
- Casts a company of actors, selects the director and designer teams.
- Directs productions.
- Attends production meetings.
- Initiates outreach for TIE (theatre in education) and touring.
- Initiates collaborations and commissions.

19

Production Manager or Technical Director

- Manages all technical aspects of the theatre and production, including health and safety.
- Employs and manages production departments and their staff.
- Attends production meetings.
- Schedules and manages on-stage fit-ups, rehearsals and the production run.

Head of Set Construction

- Manages a safe, reliable and practical workshop.
- Employs production carpentry staff.
- Orders materials.
- Attends production meetings and design presentations.
- Costs set design and meets budget constraints.
- Manages the get-in and get-out on-stage.
- Oversees the fit-up, including aspects of set flying.

Lighting and Sound Designer

- Reads the play, researches and collaborates with the director, set and costume designers.
- Attends presentations and production meetings.
- Attends rehearsals regularly.
- Designs and plots all aspects of lighting and sound for production.
- Selects equipment, hire, rig and focus, and sound tests all equipment.
- Organizes sound recordings and equipment hire.
- Instructs and manages sound and lighting staff.

Choreography and Fight Director

- Reads the play.
- Schedules appropriate rehearsals.
- Designs and directs all sequences with the cast.
- Attends production meetings.
- Collaborates with the director and design team.
- Advises design on appropriate weapons, armour and related props.
- Supervises the safe handling of weapons and props.
- Liaises fully with wardrobe and prop departments.

Head of Property Making

- Manages a safe workshop and appropriate staff.
- Orders in material.
- Collaborates with the director and design teams, and production departments.
- Attends presentations and production meetings.
- Hires and buys props for production, in addition to making.
- Manages a store for built furniture and props.
- Attends actor fittings when necessary.
- Attends rehearsals when appropriate.

Head of Scenic Art

- Manages the department staff and material needs.
- Attends to health and safety.
- Attends design presentations.
- Costs out the painted scenic elements.
- Books paint frames when applicable.
- Collaborates with carpentry over scheduling.
- Attends to all scenic paint requirements as laid out by design.
- Meets budget constraints.

Head of Wardrobe

- Manages a safe, healthy and practical workshop.
- Manages the staff for production realization.

20

- Schedules, plans and sets deadlines.
- Costs out the productions.
- Manages auxiliary departments such as the buyers, the dye room, boots and shoes, bijoux, decorations, millinery, wigs and hair, dressers and maintenance, wardrobe store.
- Organizes actor measurements and fittings.
- Collaborates with the director and designer teams.
- Attends presentations and production meetings.
- Reads the play, and researches the period.
- Orders materials.
- Manages costume realization through to opening, meets budget requirements.
- Attends rehearsals regularly.

Stage Manager
- Manages, plans and schedules all aspects of rehearsal.
- Collaborates with the director and design teams.
- Employs the deputy stage manager and assistant stage managers.

- Reads the play.
- Schedules actors' fittings in collaboration with wardrobe and props departments.
- Schedules the daily, weekly and monthly rehearsals for all cast members.
- Attends presentations and production meetings.
- Compiles and prints daily the stage management notes for all production departments.
- Plots the show in the book, and manages the running of the show on-stage through to closing night.

Musical Designer and Director
- Reads the play.
- Collaborates with the director and design team.
- Composes the music.
- Initiates the hire or buying of instruments and equipment.
- Manages the musicians.
- Schedules recordings and rehearsals.
- Attends production meetings.

3 THE DESIGNER'S RESPONSIBILITIES AND DUTIES

SCHEDULING

The process of design must be structured in order to meet a deadline – the play's opening date. All time management and planning is established by working backwards from the 'press night'. Scheduled dates reflect when the various elements of design are needed. Generally, the production period runs parallel with rehearsals. However, on large-scale productions, specific set and costume elements are made well in advance of the rehearsal period. The time allocated for the technical get-in on-stage, prior to technical rehearsals, will

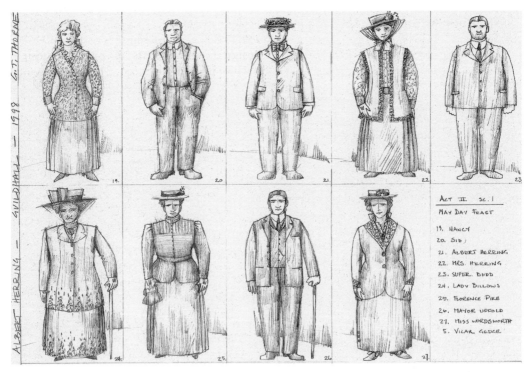

Pencil character sketches for Act II scene I of **Albert Herring.**

*A lively and charming character sketch
masterfully executed in pen and ink for*
The Three Musketeers.
Desmond Heeley. Stratford Festival Theatre

determine when things need to be completed.

Scheduling backwards from the on-stage technicals will produce crucial cut-off dates – designs coming in later will jeopardize the production. The production manager or technical director establishes these significant key deadlines.

Key Dates to Remember
1. First meeting for designer and director.
2. Presentation of preliminary sketch model and preliminary costume designs.
3. Presentation of final set model, props, and finished costume designs.
4. Presentation of technical drawings for set and props.

THE PRELIMINARY PRESENTATION

This involves the white card model. For the costume designer, viewing this model is important and it is advisable to see it as early as possible, ideally prior to the preliminary presentation. The scale model presents the architectural concept for the acting area, and how this will relate to the surrounding theatre architecture. The design provides a sense of direction for staging and blocking. A type or style of performance will be related to the set design dynamics. The proposed physical movement of the actor will lend itself to the design. The elements of costume design need to work in harmony with the elements of set design.

Tip
As director, the greatest rapport with a designer comes from saying something like 'This feels like this to me....' and then I make a gesture or a sound. They look or listen, don't laugh, then either immediately show me a sketch or a painting, or they go away and return with something that so completely represents that sound or gesture. From there, we go on to the next step: how to imaginatively and literally put that on to the stage. And from there we move to more pedestrian aspects.
Martha Henry

White card sketch model for **Patchwork Quilt.**
Polka Theatre

Preliminary sketch of front and back view for
Petra: Enemy of the People.
Stratford Festival Theatre

The Presentation

1. The white card scale model of the set sits within a black model box representing the theatre. The points of view or sightlines for the audience are demonstrated through proposed seat positions.
2. The concept for the show as a whole is presented through research, sketches or artist's renderings and costume sketches.
3. Preliminary costume sketches show a proposed silhouette for the period.
4. A costume count for numbers is outlined. The doubling of parts and omissions are included.
5. A scene breakdown chart shows actor numbers for acts and scenes.
6. Suggestion of colours and textures for costumes and set may be presented and discussed.

Steps Towards the Final Presentation

After this meeting, the director and design team will discuss how to proceed from this point. There is generally a month before the next and final presentation. The ensuing weeks of work are all about reassessing the situation in view of the comments and advice arising from the preliminary presentation.

A proposed costing should soon be available, which tends to put things into perspective. The compromises, which really begin here, are to do with constraints of space, budget and schedule. Throughout the next weeks the costume designer will re-draw; sample shop for fabric; and look into stock availability, rentals, borrowing and buying. They will plot the costume changes; meet regularly with the director and lighting designer; and keep a close eye on set design developments, especially those relating to colour. Meetings with the wardrobe department are likely to take place on a regular basis from now on.

Responsibilites Leading to The Final Presentation

1. Know the play well. Read and re-read it.
2. Research and compile documentation on the playwright, country and period. If time allows, read another play by the same author.
3. Research and compile visual information about the play's time and place. Include political, social and economic issues, season and climate, fashion and art.
4. Discuss the play thoroughly with the director. Present all research and artistic interpretations.
5. Discuss proposed budget allocations with the director.
6. Collaborate with the set and lighting designer.
7. Become familiar with the performance venue or theatre through visits and by taking photographs.
8. Learn to understand technical drawings.
9. Draw up costume charts for scene breakdowns. Note doubling of roles and quick changes.
10. Present a design for each character. Draw characters in a scene together.
11. Draw a storyboard for the scenes.
12. Draw up all costume elements.
13. Meet with the head of wardrobe to discuss developments and proposals, and budget allocation.
14. Visit costume warehouses or hire companies, take photographs.
15. Collect fabric samples from shops for each costume design.
16. Photocopy sets of finished costume designs and circulate these to other departments.
17. All costume drawings should be numbered, listing character and actor name. Identify the costume by act and scene, sign it and place in a clear portfolio sleeve for protection.
18. Identify costumes that are likely to be available from stock and those which will need to be hired or bought.

Costume designs for Idomeneo, Ilia and Idamante drawn in charcoal, pastel and chalk. Idomeneo.
Designer: Rose Bruford student, Nicki Banyard

Drawing of the imprisoned slaves and a storyboard to accompany the scene. Idomeneo.
Designer: Rose Bruford student Maggie Osborn

A fine example of a drawing which clearly expresses the designer's intention, as directed to millinery, wigs, wardrobe and the actor.
Valentine in Love for Love.
Designer: Ann Curtis. Stratford Festival Theatre

THE FINAL PRESENTATION

This meeting presents the set model and finished costume drawings. The costume designs should be in colour, show an intended choice for fabric and texture, and provide sketches of details and accessories such as wigs, hats, shoes and hand props. Based on these drawings, the production manager and head of wardrobe (along with the department heads), will calculate a fairly accurate breakdown of costing. When necessary, discussions are organized between the designer and all departments to ensure a balanced costing. These meetings are important for the designer as staff experiences often contribute largely to material choice and construction methods.

Tip

I believe that the first fitting is the time when I learn the most about my part. By that time one has rehearsed long enough to be ready for a nudge or even a push toward the completed vision. I use fittings to tell me things about character that have not yet penetrated my body or perhaps my mind. I use the first fitting carefully and find when I go back into rehearsals, I am always substantially further along. A fitting needs a rhythm; much detailed work can be done, but it needs the awareness from the wardrobe department that this is the first or second meeting of the actor with the outward personification of their character. There must be a union between actor and character on that day, the momentum during the fitting should enable this to happen. It's a blind date: you've seen the picture – and now you want to know if the two of you will get along.

Martha Henry

The Presentation

1. Completed drawings for all characters, with details of acts and scenes.
2. A breakdown chart of costumes for each scene.
3. Drawings for hats, wigs, shoes, head-dress and masks.
4. Sketches for accessories such as bags, umbrellas and jewellery.
5. Fabric samples for each costume.
6. Breakdown of stock, rentals, buys and makes.

Planning and preparing in advance helps the designer meet the deadlines. Time-management is an essential ingredient. Aim to get the most out of the weeks prior to

27

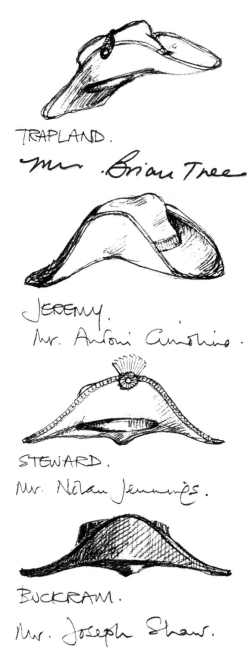

TRAPLAND.

mr. Brian Tree

JEREMY.

Mr. Antoni Cimolino.

STEWARD.

Mr. Nolan Jennings.

BUCKRAM.

Mr. Joseph Shaw.

The type of sketch which the millinery department love to receive in addition to the costume sketch. Love for Love. *Designer: Ann Curtis. Stratford Festival Theatre*

presentations. The more you can achieve in terms of research, design and presentation; the better prepared you will be to engage in the production process.

SHOPPING FOR FABRIC SAMPLES

When fabric shopping be sure to take your working 'bible' (see page 36); a conveniently sized waterproof portfolio for the original drawings; a hand staple gun and a pen. All drawings should be individually protected with a clear plastic or acetate cover.

Shopping for fabric is both exciting and exhausting. Free samples may amount to no more than a sliver or mere snippet – small samples are a disadvantage when the feel of the fabric matters in relation to its drape and natural weight. It is advisable to staple each sample immediately into your binder together with a note of the shop's name, the fabric content, the price per metre and how much there is in stock. Keep one page for each character in the play. By stapling the samples along the right-hand edge, the page to the left of the sample is available for all notes.

Initial shopping trips will identify the readily available retail choices. However, many companies offer a wide selection of stock ranges to order. Bulk buying may prove an advantage financially.

Wardrobe will generally put aside a reasonable amount of time to shop. However, the choice can often be overwhelming and it is easy to overlook a very suitable fabric. After several good days of sampling it is advisable to sit in the studio and study the collection with all the drawings before you. A little time and distance gives you a fresh look at things.

Fabric is generally manufactured with one side being the 'right' side, the preferred front. However, it is quite possible that you will prefer the back and will choose it as your garment face.

When sorting through the samples be sure to consider how the fabric will behave once made up and its characteristics under lighting. The appropriate departments should be consulted before any firm choice of fabric is made.

Making decisions gets the show in motion. Once you have chosen a fabric, all further choices should be made with reference to it. It is important to keep a relation between the parts, so they add up to an overall vision. Texture and colour play very important parts of the equation here, so too does weight and quality of fabric in relation to the time, place and season of the play.

FABRIC CONTENT AND CHARACTERISTICS

Manufacturers and producers of cloth provide a content description for their textiles, which may include cleaning instructions. It is recommended that you inquire into fibre content and the material care. Most retailers know what they order and sell, although market stall holders may be less well informed. Whenever uncertainty as to fibre content arises, you should do a burn test (*see* page 31).

Nowadays, garments are required by law to include details of fibre content and recommended instructions for cleaning. Look through your own wardrobe and note the differences as indicated on the labels.

The characteristics of fibre vary according to how it is manufactured. Fibre blends and the manufactured twist produces a large range of differing yarns. The method and type of weave along with the finishing treatments create uniquely different fabrics. What we observe from looking at and responding to a fabric is affected by these manufactured characteristics. Our eye tells us something about the tactile sensation. We are affected by how light interacts with material. We feel something for the weight of material. We respond to the sculptural aspects of fabric. Our senses fall prey to being seduced by the veiling quality or restrictive nature or the movement of fabric on the body. That which catches our eye should be carefully observed and questioned. We may have an aversion to a fabric determined by the way it feels. How often have you purchased a garment because you like the feel of the material? How often have you considered a purchase for what the material reflects or says to the onlooker? How often are both aspects considered before purchase?

Sensations vary for every type of fabric. The smell of fabric may affect your appreciation for it. Natural fleece yarns, hair fibres, plant and vegetable yarns may well attract through the characteristic of having a smell. These moisture-absorbent fibres smell when damp or wet.

Textile manufacturers continually try to surprise us through innovation. The re-invention of fabric may give a garment a new, more practical use. Denim is a fabric that has been re-invented several times. There are now denims of pure 100 per cent cotton, cotton mixed with man-made fibre, and man-made synthetic denims (lycra denim is such a fabric).

DYING FABRIC

When colours and patterns prove difficult to find, it is likely that the solution will be to dye a fabric. With appropriate dye room facilities and a skilled technician, most things become possible. The dye room will require large enough fabric samples to allow them some scope for trial and error. Purchase the minimum cut length, usually 10cm (4in). The width will give them the measure they need to sample dye.

29

THE BURN TEST

FIBRE	APPROACHING FLAME	IN FLAME	REMOVED FROM FLAME	ODOUR	ASH
Cotton	Scorches: ignites quickly	Burns quickly: yellow flame	Continues to burn rapidly: has afterglow	Burning paper	Light and feathery grey ash. If mercerized, ash is black
Linen	Scorches: ignites quickly	Burns less quickly than cotton: yellow flame	Continues to burn: has afterglow	Burning paper	Light and feathery grey ash
Silk	Smoulders	Burns slowly: sputters and melts	Burns with difficulty: ceases to flame	Burning hair	Round, shiny black bead easy to crush
Wool	Smoulders: ignites slowly	Burns slowly: with small flickering flame: sizzles and curls	Ceases to flame	Burning hair: stronger odour than silk	Crisp dark ash: round, irregular bead, easy to crush.
Rayon	Scorches: ignites quickly	Burns more quickly than cotton: bright yellow flame	Continues to burn: has no afterglow	Burning paper	Light and feathery ash
Acetate	Fuses away from flame: turns black	Blazes and burns quickly: sputters, melts, and drips like burning tar	Continues to melt and burn	Vinegar	Hard black ash: irregular bead, difficult to crush
Nylon	Fuses and shrinks away from flame	Melts, then burns slowly	Flame ceases then dies out	Celery	Round, hard greyish bead, will not crush
Polyester	Fuses and shrinks away from flame	Melts, then burns slowly	Burns with difficulty	Sweetish	Round, hard greyish bead, will not crush
Acrylic	Fuses and shrinks away from flame	Flames rapidly: sputters and melts	Continues to melt and burn	Burning meat	Irregular, hard, black bead, will not crush
Modacrylic	Fuses and shrinks away from flame	Melts and burns slowly	Ceases to burn	Sweet	Irregular, hard, black bead, will not crush
Spandex	Fuses in flame	Melts and burns	Continues to melt and burn	Sharp, bitter	Soft, light, black ash
Rubber	Smoulders	Melts and shrivels away from flame	Ceases to burn	Intense, pungent	Irregular, hard, black bead

BEOWULF REHEARSAL SCHEDULE
(Rehearsal will generally take place in St.Winefrides, w/u = warm ups)

Mon	30/3	10.00	Co. call, read thru, model box & costumes with staff, singing
Tue	31/3	09.00	Company meeting, w/u, puppetry, blocking Act 1
Wed	1/4	9.45	w/u, blocking Act 1, (publicity photo call)
Thu	2/4	9.45	w/u, blocking Act 1
Fri	3/4	9.45	w/u, blocking Act 1, coffee w/staff & pm puppetry
Sat	4/4	9.45	w/u, puppetry (till 14.00)
Sun	5/4	FREE	
Mon	6/4	9.45	w/u, am run through Act 1(off books)pm blocking Act 2
Tue	7/4	9.45	(company meeting), w/u, blocking Act 2
Wed	8/4	9.45	w/u, blocking act 2
Thu	9/4	9.45	w/u, blocking Act 2
Fri	10/4	9.45	w/u, am run Act 1& pm run-through Act 2 (off books)
Sat	11/4	9.45	w/u, run through Act 1&2 (till 14.00)
Sun	12/4	FREE	HAPPY EASTER
Mon	13/4	FREE	HAPPY EASTER
Tue	14/4	9.45	(Company meeting),w/u, slow clarifying blocking
Wed	15/4	9.45	w/u, clarifying blocking, pm 'run-through'
Thu	16/4	9.45	w/u, clarifying blocking, pm 'run-through'
Fri	17/4	9.45	w/u, run-through, costume parade
Sat	18/4	9.30	w/u, run through (till 13.00)
Sun	19/4	FREE	
Mon	20/4	10.00	w/u, rehearsal (not on stage)
Tue	21/4	10.00	(Sound check @ 9.30) TECHNICAL DAY (a long day, 'till 23.00! bring grub)
Wed	22/4	10.00	Continuation of the tech if needs be 14.00 1st dress rehearsal with photo call 19.00 2nd dress rehearsal (another long day-again until 23.00)
Thu	23/4	14.00	OPENING PREVEW 19.00 TEACHER'S PREVIEW
Fri	24/4	10.30	FIRST PERFORMANCE

Warm up start from 9.45 followed by a vocal warm-up. Coffee break is at 11.30, lunch at 13.00 and tea at 15.45. Normally rehearsals finish at 17.30 with an option till 18.00. On Saturdays rehearsals will tend to be from 9.45 to 14.00.

Once the show opens please look at the performance schedule issued from the box office (releases on the last Friday of rehearsals) for further details. Please note that the following ten days of performances are still liable to be 'improved' upon and any 'watch this space' or * or time after a performance may be taken up with a rehearsal session.

We also have a close-at-hand policy with 'special needs' audiences and ask for some actors, time permitting, to be available to talk with groups after a performance.

Safety Procedure
Please read the various 'Fire & General Emergency' notices and make yourselves aware of the safety precautions in operation. Stage management will organise a fire drill during the run.

A rehearsal schedule for Beowulf, starting with the first day of rehearsal and the read through of the play. Polka Theatre

A corset and calico toile or mock up ready for the first fitting. Stratford Festival Theatre

Always make decisions concerning dyed fabric samples when they are completely dry. Consider the colour relationship to other costume fabrics in the scene or act. Keep a sample of the original fabric in the working 'bible': alongside this, staple in the dyed sample and note the particulars of the dye. Note any care and cleaning recommendations provided by the dye room technicians.

Some man-made fibres will not dye. Fabric often has a mixed content, so protect yourself and sample dye before buying any lengths of fabric. Dye all fabric before giving it to the wardrobe cutters or tailors.

STOCK AND HIRED COSTUMES

When you need to incorporate stock or hired costumes into your designs consider the following points:

1. Check first the percentage of stock costuming as proposed by the wardrobe department. This is usually done at an early stage, before designing on paper begins.

2. Visit the stock warehouse or rental house to see the selection available.
3. Note the particulars concerning the colour range, choice of sizes, patterns, quality and finish.
4. Ascertain which other garments and accessories come included in the price of the costume rental.
5. Photograph in colour the selection you propose to use, for your own and the director's reference.
6. Whenever possible, select more than one costume for each character. Make an arrangement to return the others after the fittings.
7. Consider taking half a costume, such as a doublet or bodice, and request wardrobe make the breeches or skirt. This helps blend stock with newly made costumes, thus keeping the overall look in better harmony.
8. With a theatre's stock costumes you may have more licence to cut and re-assemble.
9. Draw stock costumes on characters when you design the show. Incorporate them into the look of the show.

FROM PRESENTATION TO PRODUCTION

Once the final presentation is completed, the production process begins. The production period may well start before the rehearsal period. Day one of rehearsal is another presentation, this time for the acting company. Because this is the first read through of the play, all departments are generally present. The presentation is the first glimpse for the actors of what the show will look like as a whole, as well as how they will be dressed. There is a presentation by the director then one by the designer. The introduction is kept brief yet informative, it concerns the decisions already made and how these balance with the

32

Chorus for Idomeneo.
Designer: Rose Bruford student Pam Glew

proposed sense of direction. The next time the costume designer meets with the actor will be either in rehearsal, or more importantly through the fittings.

FITTINGS

Each and every fitting is of significance for the actor, designer and wardrobe staff. Fittings are limited in number, so the time spent together, being short, must prove informative, constructive and reassuring to the actor. There are often many department heads at the fitting so as to cover all aspects of costuming. The first fitting may be with a constructed mock-up costume made of calico. Cutting the show fabric comes after the shape, fit and proportions are balanced out in the mock-up.

Actors have real concerns about costume, so this is the time to encourage them to speak their minds. All concerns are a matter of importance. Discuss the physical movements being explored in rehearsal, the development of attitude in character, and the comfort and ease of the costume. The next opportunity for a fitting will be in the show fabric, with more completed elements from other departments. These fittings are collaborations, yet the main focus must be on how the actor feels when wearing the costume.

THE COSTUME DESIGN SKETCH

The Drawing as Reference

The drawing is the first stage in making a costume and often needs to be assessed by several different departments in order to establish the best way to proceed. Getting the garment to the stage of fitting the tailor's dummy and then on to the actor is an involved process.

Throughout the process of realization, the designer and wardrobe department consider issues affecting the shape, weight, and overall effect of the costume relative to how it fits the actor. In addition, new demands may now be made as a result of issues arising from rehearsal. The costume may need to be adapted to accommodate the actor's movements, quick changes, and physical stress. These factors may prove a challenge to your original design. Nevertheless, through well-considered decisions with regard to fabric and construction methods, the costume can retain the essence of the sketched intention.

It is recommended that colour features as an essential design element in all your sketches. These original drawings are passed on to wardrobe, where they should remain throughout the whole of production. Copies

33

*Chorus of Priests and Idamante in the
sacrifice scene of* Idomeneo.
Designer: Rose Bruford student Anna Jeffery

should be made for reference use only. The dye
room and fabric painters should always refer to
the originals. The designer keeps copies in the
show 'bible'.

The Purpose of Costume Drawings

1 For the designer, the drawings are a
representation of the ideas and intentions
discussed with the director. They describe
the concept for the show as a whole.
2 The drawings are a comprehensive look at all
the characters, which should be well
developed and have accompanying
information to inform the viewer. Each
drawing needs to have the name of the
character, the scene and act, the actor's
name, the designer's name and the name of
the production.
3 The drawings describe the character in

form, proportion and costume detail. The
information is conveyed to the observer
through confident handling of line, shape,
colour, texture, pattern and value.
4 Each character should have a drawing.
These are frequently designed with the
actor's physical stature in mind.
5 Drawings serve to inform every member
of staff employed in realizing the
costume. They are of value to all
wardrobe departments, the props
department and the buyers. The drawing
or accompanying sketches describe the
understructure or foundation for making.
The breakdown or ageing of a costume
should be incorporated into the drawing.
6 The collection of drawings should
accompany the designer and buyer on all
shopping trips. They are the reference for
fabric sampling, material and accessory
buying.
7 Within the rehearsal room a collection of
copies are hung for reference purposes. Actors,
stage management, the director, choreo-
grapher and fight director will frequently need
to refer to them.
8 Throughout the fittings, the drawings serve as
a goal to which all involved are aiming. The
sketches are always present, frequently
attached to the wall alongside the long mirror.
9 When a production is completed, the drawings
serve as an archive. Copies of the drawings,
along with photographs of the actors in
costume, are placed into the 'bible', a record of
the costumed production. The 'bible' contains
all information on fabrics and dying, trims and
accessories. This 'bible' can be of great interest
and importance historically.

Accompanying Drawings

These drawings serve to inform various
wardrobe departments. Drawings may show
several views, such as the front, sides and
back.

Character act and scene breakdown chart for *Albert Herring*

ACT 1
SCENE 1   LADY BILLOW'S MANOR HOUSE
LADY BILLOWS
FLORENCE
MISS WORDSWORTH
VICOR GEDGE
SUPER BUDD
MAYOR UPFOLD

ACT 1
SCENE 2   HERRING'S GREENGROCERY
                                           SAME DAY

EMMIE
CIS
HARRY
SID
ALBERT
NANCY
FLORENCE
MRS. HERRING
ALL

ACT 2
SCENE 1   MARGUEE MAY-DAY

FLORENCE
SID
MISS WORDSWORTH WITH EMMIE, CIS, HARRY
SUPER BUDD
MRS HERRING
MAYOR UPFOLD
VICAR GEDGE
LADY BILLOWS
ALBERT
NANCY

ACT 2
SCENE 2   HERRING'S GREENGROCERY
LATER THAT EVENING
ALBERT
SID
NANCY
MRS HERRING

Costume drawing for Idomeneo.
Designer: Rose Bruford student Nina McDonagh

1 Hair and wig styles
2 Millinery
3 Neckwear and ties
4 Jewellery
5 Footwear
6 Overcoats

THE WORKING 'BIBLE'

As mentioned previously, this is the record of the process from drawing through to finished garment. The amount of use this binder gets demands that it be both practical in its layout and of a sturdy nature – a hardcover, A4 ring binder is ideal. It should contain the following:

• Blank sheets of A4 hole-punched paper.
• Coloured index dividers, one for each costume.
• A copy of the detailed costume-breakdown page for each costume.
• A photocopy of each costume drawing.

Organize the order with the principals first, followed by supporting roles, non-speaking roles and extras. If you wish to file all the costumes for one character together,

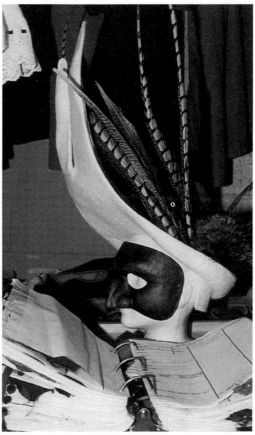

The working 'bible' with characters' costume breakdown pages inserted. Attached are swatches, dyed fabric samples and trim, with notes on all costume elements.
Mask and hat: Debra Hanson.
Stratford Festival Theatre

include a separate, detailed costume-breakdown page for each costume, even when parts of the costume remain throughout. Label the costume-breakdown pages clearly with act and scene numbers.

Staple on to the blank pages all fabric samples and note such details as where and when it was purchased; price per metre or yard; the fabric content; and cleaning or

Character's costume breakdown page for the 'Bible'.

COSTUME BREAKDOWN   CHARACTER

WIG/HAIR   ACT & SCENE

                                     ACTORS NAME

MILLINERY   PHOTOGRAPH

COSTUME PIECES

ACCESSORIES

UNDERPINNINGS

HOSE

SHOES/FOOTWEAR

BIJOUX

DRESSER NOTES/LAUNDRY-CLEANING NOTES

MISCELLANEOUS

laundry requirements – this is especially important with dyed and hand-painted costumes. Include all fabrics used in underclothes such as corsets, petti-coats, chemise and jabot fabrics, and those for millinery trim. Staple in the chosen dyed sample, include alongside all dye notes. Include trim, fringing, braid, ribbon, lining fabrics, padding materials, button samples, lace, appliqué or hand-painting samples and note details.

DUTIES AND RESPONSIBILITIES OF THE ASSISTANT COSTUME DESIGNER

Function

Responsible to the designer, the design assistant should be able to take over a show if for any reason the designer is unable to continue or has to be away for an extended length of time. A design assistant should be able to make appropriate design decisions if the designer is unable to for any reason. The design assistant should act as a visual co-ordinator between the various production departments and the designer. Assistants are expected to research the period and know the play thoroughly.

Duties

1. Photocopy and distribute drawings of costumes, wigs, hats, shoes, jewellery and other accessories to:
- head of wardrobe
- production manager
- stage management
- wig department
- decorators
- millinery department
- dye department
- boot and shoe department
- jewellery department
- buyers
- warehouse manager
2. Arrange for the design sketches to be photographed for archive records.
3. Ensure that the sketches and drawings are in portfolio sleeves.
4. Number and label all sketches.
5. Organize the 'bible' to include:
- samples of selected fabrics with source, price and width; dye samples
- details of underpinnings such as corsets, underwear, hoops, bustles, rolls
- details of costume pieces including millinery, shoes, skirts, dresses, blouses, jackets, coats
- accessories such as gloves, hand-kerchiefs, umbrellas, jewellery
- wig and facial hair details
- photographs of the actors in costume
- lists of garment pieces from stock, made, hired, bought
- lists of underclothes from stock, made, hired, bought
- footwear details
6. Draw up and distribute to department heads, lists and notes concerning:
- characters in acts and scenes
- material breakdown and ageing
- costume changes
- garments which require special handling due to breakdown and dye, including maintenance, washing and pressing restrictions, dry cleaning requirements
7. Co-ordinate with stage management to:
- find rehearsal props, costumes and accessories
- collect information which needs passing on from director to designer
- keep stage management aware of the designer's movements and shopping schedule
- schedule fittings
8. Co-ordinate with wardrobe to:
- provide tights (hose) and appropriate

Character's costume breakdown chart
for *Albert Herring*

LADY BILLOWS

ACT SC. 1

CORSET
PETTICOAT
BUM ROLL
BLOUSE (High Collar)
SKIRT
INDOOR LOOSE JACKET (Knit)
HOSE
SHOES
HANDKERCHIEF
HAIR-UP

ACT 1 SC. 2

SAME AS SC.1 ADD:
COAT (Full Length) WITH PERSIAN LAMB TRIM
(Cuffs & Collar)
HAT WITH VEIL
GLOVES
WALKING STICK

ACT 2 SC.1 MARQUEE

SUIT-SUMMER WEIGHT STRIPED
BLOUSE # 1 IF POSSIBLE
SAME BASIC'S AS ACT 1
HAT # 2

ACT 3

SAME AS ACT 1 SC2
HAT # 1 WITH ADDITIONAL CROW PLUMBS
POSSIBLE UMBRELLA

FLORENCE PIKE

ACT 1 SC.1

MAIDS DRESS
COLLAR - HIGH DOWN TURNED
CUFFS - WHITE 1 1/2"
CORSET
PETTICOAT
HOSE
SHOES
APRON # 1 WAISTED
APRON # FULL
WATCH
HAIR - UP

ACT 1 SC.2

BASIC # 1 ADD:
COAT - LONG
HAT - FELT/WOOL
GLOVES
UMBRELLA

ACT 2 SC.1 MARQUEE

SKIRT
JACKET (Short)
BLOUSE
BASIC'S AS IN ACT 1
HAT #2 STRAW BOATER

ACT 3

BASIC AS IN ACT 1 SC.2

DESIGN: GARY THORNE

Provisional prop list for *Albert Herring*

(White Card Model Meeting)

NOTES:

- This props list has been prepared in advance for the purposes of the white card model meeting. As such is only provisional and will be added to before and during rehearsal (though not greatly I suspect).

- Consultation on each and every item is essential. In the first place this should be with the Designer (Gary Thorne) and then subsequently with the Director (Thomas de Mallet Burgess).

- The deadline for above list (or substitutes) is first day of rehearsal). It is essential that all props (or clearly marked substitutes) are available from the first day of rehearsal including substitute items of costume.

- The production will be set in Loxford, a small market-town in East Suffolk during April and May circa 1914. All items must conform to the period unless specified.

PROPS (including costume substitutes required for rehearsal):

ACT 1. Scene 1.

Breakfast things for one on a tray
Duster
Riding crop (for a woman) and dirty riding clothes (full set)-
Laundry basket filled with dirty linen
Large household book and pencil
Small tables
Small table clock
Six identical chairs
Hats sticks or umbrellas for Miss Wordswoth, Vicar, Budd, Mayor Pocket watches for Miss Wordsworth, Super. Budd, Mayor
Glasses for Florence (pince-nez), Miss Wordsworth, Vicar
Small pocket notebooks and pencils for Miss Wordsworth, Vicar, Super. Budd, Mayor
Walking stick for Lady Billows
Sherlock Holmes pipe for Super. Budd and tobacco pouch. Small side table with practical tea service for 6 (including cups, saucers, spoons, plates suger bowl, cakes,napkins etc.)

Doublet on a tailor's dummy. A useful aid to working on the costume without the actor. Designer: Lewis Brown
Stratford Festival Theatre

basics for fittings
• label accessory boxes for each character
• select stock costumes for fittings
• keep an accurate record of the stock articles required, notes on alterations being made, and dye, painting, and breakdown particulars

• return all unused stock costumes
• prepare for and attend all actor fittings and ensure the fitting rooms are left tidy
• take notes at fittings, rehearsals, technical dress rehearsals, photocalls and previews
• distribute such notes to the wardrobe cutters and tailors, and other wardrobe departments
• note the time factor for getting in ordered material, trim and accessories
• assist the buyer for wardrobe in making correct orders
• assist in the fabric stock room with labelling each bolt of fabric with the name of the actor and character and note yard or metre lengths
• note requests made by departments and deadlines for decision making
9. Write out the dresser sheets.
10. Assist in the preparation of repair kits for the wardrobe dressers.
11. Inform wardrobe of costume fire-proofing needs.
12. Assist in breakdown of costumes when required.
13. Attend buying trips.

4   THE PLAYWRIGHT AND THE PLAY

P laywrights skilfully shape ideas into subject matter, language, character and action, to create forms of expression. The play has been crafted to express points of view. Characters represent ideas and attitudes, and it is through their relationships that the dynamics of plot and dramatic action moves towards an end.

The playwright and play are subject to assessment and analysis. Professional criticism fills the bookshop shelves. Some of it proves a useful accompaniment for studying a play. Reviews of a performance, mainly in respect of the original staging, can also be revealing and informative.

The playwright's interpretation of an event or a situation is personal – that is, of their imagination. As all plays are, to some extent, an original creation, any formal approach to analysis becomes complex. It may prove practical to make an analysis through comparison with another of the playwright's works.

The structure and language of the play in performance may appear to be lifelike, although this is rarely, if ever, the case. Dialogue is the invention of the playwright. The resulting discourse is therefore contrived and its staging subject to the conventions of theatre, which has much to do with illusion making. To stage a play the theatre needs people with imagination, practised in the skills and crafts of making theatre.

Seasonal wear circa 1960. Barbara Bryne as Kath in **Entertaining Mr Sloane.**
Director: David William. Lighting: John Munro. Stratford Festival Theatre.
Courtesy of the Stratford Festival Archives

42

A play is written to be performed, like musical composition. Plays need actors, and the actor requires an audience. Interaction is all important: it creates a relationship, and what the actor needs above all else is a relationship with the audience. To be successful, the performance must capture and maintain the audience's interest and imagination. When performance succeeds in engaging the audience's interest, the craft of theatre is working in support of the play. Innovation in both design and performance are necessary to maintain interest over a duration of time. A play has an ever shifting nature, and design serves this progressive nature, from its beginning through to its end.

The Play

Structure

The play's structure is an essential part of its character. Structure holds together the progression of ideas and relationship. The creative team looks at structure to better understand the play's dynamics. Structure is seen to shape itself through scenes and acts towards an aim, the ending.

In Alan Ayckbourn's *Intimate Exchange* the structure has variables, which offer themselves up as eight plays within one. The variables make it appear that the actor has choices, which in turn affect where the play will go. *Events on a Hotel Terrace* and *A Game of*

Finished costume sketch in designer gouache.
Barbara Bryne in Entertaining Mr Sloane.
Stratford Festival Theatre

Finished costume sketch in pencil and watercolour for **Enemy of the People.**
Stratford Festival Theatre

A costume that captures and maintains an audience's interest. Designer: Lewis Brown
Stratford Festival Theatre

Vibrant pattern and colour for Harlequin.
Designer: Lewis Brown
Stratford Festival Theatre

Golf help illustrate the enjoyable nature of playing about with structure. In the first scene of both plays, Cecily leaves the house and enters the garden (an on-stage garden setting). She then may either pause for a cigarette or choose to carry on to the garden shed. If Cecily stops for a smoke, she hears the door bell and returns inside to answer it. However, if she instead carries on to the shed (without having a smoke), she does not hear the door bell and her life goes off in a very different direction.

Monologue

The monologue involves one actor before an audience. The recounting of experience is a form of story telling. To sustain audience interest, the monologue requires the visual support of elements of scenery suggesting location and a designed costume. Without such support the production may look like stand-up comedy.

Alan Bennett's *Talking Heads* is a collection of monologues, written for specific actors. Their staging should give enough visual information to enlighten the audience on place and character, without over emphasis.

In *Search for Signs of Intelligent Life in the Universe* by Jane Wagner, there are twelve characters, all of which are played by one actress. The play's structure is such that no costume changes can occur. It is also inappropriate for the actress to use costume elements to suggest character. Instead she stands alone, in a costume which needs to look unobtrusive yet interesting, one which is more unmemorable than memorable. The setting needs to support a sense of all of the locations, and lighting and sound play dynamic roles throughout the performance.

Duologue

The duologue is two actors on-stage, their interaction creates a relationship dependent on a shared experience. The characters perform within a designed space and dress in costume. Unless there is a major time change within the play, it is unlikely for costume changes to occur.

Language

Dialogue between characters is usually presented as direct conversation or discourse. Styles of language characteristically differ depending on period and country. Discourse is contrived, it is the invention of the playwright.

Naturalistic discourse when found in Shakespeare appears as direct language and is presented as natural speech. This mode of language sits comfortably with its audience.Example: In *The Taming Of The Shrew*, Sly is introduced being thrown out of the pub for being drunk and breaking glasses that he cannot pay for. This familiar and quite likeable character dresses as a tinker or vagabond might: the texture, age and poor quality of his clothes highlight his very simple nature. Waking from a drunken slumber he tries to identify himself before a crowd of aristocratic strangers.

SLY: Am not I Christopher Sly, old Sly's son of Burton-heath, by birth a pedlar, by education a cardmaker, by transmutation a bed-herd, and now by present profession a tinker? Ask Marion Hacket, the fat ale-wife of Wincot, if she knows me not. If she say I am not fourteen pence on the score for sheer ale, score me up for the lyingest knave in Christendom.

A trick is being played on Sly: he has awoken to find that he appears to have become the lord of the manor. A new guise is now presented which complements the surrounding splendour. All the household are in on the game. Sly's naturalistic language is in marked contrast to the aristocratic speech of the others. Before long Sly is sounding out of

An expressive character on a black background. White pencil with gouache and lettering. Corrine Koslo in Search for Signs of Intelligent Life in the Universe.
Alberta Theatre Projects

45

The Narrator stands out to the left of the group in light-coloured clothing. She plays in and out of the play throughout.
Beowulf. *Director: Roman Stefanski. Lighting: Neil Fraser. Polka Theatre*

character and imitating those surrounding him.

SLY:
Am I a Lord and have I such a Lady?
Or do I dream? Or have I dreamed till now?
I do not sleep. I see, I hear, I speak.
I smell sweet savours and I feel soft things.
Upon my life, I am a Lord indeed,
And not a tinker, nor Christopher Sly.
Well, bring our lady hither to our sight,
And once again a pot o'th'smallest ale.

Literary Manner

Dialogue mode of a literary manner places the drama within a heightened style of language. In Sheridan's *The Rivals*, the language of Mrs Malaprop satirizes the manners of the period. Sheridan plays with the hypocrisy of the time to great comic and ironic effect as the society it reflects was very much that of the select audience which attended.

Accent and Dialect

Some plays consist of regional dialect. In these circumstances, actors, directors and designers will find themselves at a disadvantage if they do not fully research local dialects, colloquialisms and accents. Handbooks accompanying the play may assist. Dialect adds texture, and costume can support regional differences.

Action

Action is considered to be a result of discourse. The motivation for action comes through what characters think and say. A protagonist who is seeking revenge will be surrounded by reactions, some of which are significant, others of less importance. How characters gesture, move, and react physically will make the costume appear to come to life. Fabric and its drape, its characteristics for taking on an imposed shape, and how it moves is of real concern when being applied to character. Anticipating how the character will move, and what attitudes they reflect, determines which types of materials are chosen. Directors encourage actors to justify and reason out why they move and initiate action.

around and relate to them. It is crucial that the audience is able to clearly follow and understand the protagonist's character, which may be highly complex.

Zastrozzi, for example, is the master criminal of Europe, an aristocratic cold-blooded murderer, driven by revenge. *Zastrozzi* by George

Robert Bockstael playing Zastrozzi.
Director: Bob White.
Lighting: Harry Frehner. Alberta Theatre Projects.
Photo: Trudie Lee

THE CHARACTERS

The Protagonist

The protagonist is the principal or lead character, who carries the main plot of the play forward, inciting or provoking other characters to react through their words and action. For the audience, the protagonist is the main focus: all events and actions revolve

The protagonist Dr Stockman and his family
in Enemy Of The People.
Director: Martha Henry. Setting: Phillip Silver.
Lighting: Louise Guinand.
Stratford Festival Theatre. Courtesy of the
Stratford Festival Archives

F Walker is set in Italy at the end of the nineteenth century. Political change is affecting and killing off the 'old rule'. To avenge his mother's death, Zastrozzi focuses on an artist, a painter who is the personification of the new age of enlightened liberalism. Obsessed with discipline and evil, driven by threats to his privileged birthright, Zastrozzi targets the middle classes. The protagonist and his accomplices provoke, challenge and wreak havoc.

Synge's *Playboy Of The Western World* introduces us to Christy Mahon, a runaway farm boy who finds refuge in a remote Irish pub. Mahon spins a tale in which he boasts of murdering his father. Although Mahon becomes something of a hero to the local girls, the community reacts differently, which leads to a surprising and dramatic end to the events.

Protagonists include:
* King Lear, Julius Caesar, Henry V, Hamlet, Macbeth (Shakespeare)
* Nora in *A Doll's House*, Ellida in *Lady from the Sea*, Dr Stockman in *Enemy of the People* (Ibsen)
* Joan of Arc (George Bernard Shaw)

The antagonist (seated) and supporting character. David Storch as Verezzi (seated) and Wes Tritter as Victor in Zastrozzi.
Director: Bob White. Lighting: Harry Frehner. Alberta Theatre Projects. Photo: Trudie Lee

* Bernarda in *The House of Bernarda Alba* (Garcia Lorca)
* Uncle Vanya (Chekhov)

The Antagonist

The antagonist, who may have either good or bad character traits, acts as the main opposition to the protagonist, serving to contrast and challenge the main thrust of ideas. The role of the antagonist may be significant either in terms of speech or intricately woven into the scenes and acts.

Antagonists include:
* The principal antagonist to Peter Pan is Captain Hook.
* The antagonist to Othello is his right-hand man Iago.
* For Bernarda Alba, her antagonist proves to be her own daughter Adela.
* For Cinderella the antagonists are her two ugly step-sisters.

Leading Characters

The term is associated with those characters, which through the action of the play, achieve some form of development in character. They may either rise or fall in status and display change as the play moves forward, which is brought about through their understanding and acquiring new forms of knowledge. They are affected by the ideas and actions of both the protagonist and antagonist.

Supporting Characters

The supporting characters generally serve to emphasize or strengthen issues that are raised by the principal or leading characters. Holding on to belief and doctrine, they add dimension and force to the plot associated with unchanging views, often demonstrating a resistance towards changing ideals.

Supporting characters, by their very nature, have less sense of history and direction. The

New meets old in Knight of the Burning Pestle. *The greengrocer and wife with apprentice interrupt the play's proceedings in an attempt to liven things up. The cast on-stage at the Tom Patterson.*
Directors: Bernard Hopkins and Pat Galloway. Lighting: Kevin Fraser. Stratford Festival Theatre. Courtesy of the Stratford Festival Archives

creative team may need to flesh these characters out through developing subtext, which is used as background information for the actor to help him develop the role through an understanding of how his character fits into plot and location.

The Stereotypical Character

The appearance of a uniform that displays rank, power or profession causes something in us all to sit up and pay attention. Uniforms call attention to themselves, as both a symbol and representation of authority. Our reactions on seeing a uniform will vary, depending upon our own relationships and experiences. On stage, a uniform has the power to stand alone without words. Abuse of a uniform can cause waves of reaction.

In Jean Genet's *The Balcony*, the setting is a brothel. The clients, driven by their most private compulsions, achieve erotic and power fulfilment through fantasy, by dressing up in the uniforms of a general, a bishop or a judge. Genet clearly intends these characters to be played in an exaggerated fashion. Each costume is to be larger than life, with the help of 'buskins' about 50cm (20in) in height, attached to the feet.. Genet recommends the costumes be excessive yet not unrecognizable.

In William Congreve's delightful comedy *Love for Love*, Sir Sampson introduces a lawyer. His appearance is brief, hence being introduced as 'Brief Buckram the Lawyer'. Buckram is called upon to authorize Valentine's signature on papers drawn up by Valentine's father, Sir

49

Sampson. Valentine feigns madness and Buckram therefore dismisses the signature as invalid. Valentine describes Buckram as wearing black, and he asks whether Buckram 'carries his conscience withoutside?' Buckram shys away in fear of anything seemingly abnormal or irregular 'for it is not good in law!' The short yet dramatic time when Buckram is on stage requires that he has an immediate impact upon the audience. Buckram's uniform needs to help describe his extremely conservative nature, and to make him look something of the odd man out in this situation – Valentine is clever and romantic while Sir Sampson is eccentric and quite neurotic.

The Chorus

A chorus stands to represent ideas collectively – they are frequently a community or society of attitude, without individuals. The aim of the design must, therefore, be to unify and harmonize, so they appear as a collective. This

Front and back views for sailor Horster in **Enemy of the People.**

A delightful sketch with interesting wig and accessories. Buckram in Love For Love.
Designer: Ann Curtis. Stratford Festival Theatre

can be achieved through unifying silhouette, colour, texture and pattern. A chorus may consist of subdivided groups with leaders. Design needs to retain the image of a group whilst allowing for touches of variation or variations on a theme. The aim is to create enough interest visually to differentiate, yet retain a unifying look.

The audience's eye should wander freely, yet be continually encouraged to view the chorus as a collective. In Lorca's *House of Bernarda Alba*, a very large crowd of women mourners enter the house. They wear full black Andulusian mourning dress, including lace, shawls and fans. This group is a powerful symbol of community, performing ritual and tradition. The impact must be overwhelming.

Pencil sketches for the Lost Boys. Variations on a theme. Peter Pan

The cast of Lost Boys with Peter Pan and Wendy (lying wounded behind). Director: Michael Winter. Setting: Vikie Le Sache. Lighting: Jim Bowman. Mercury Theatre, Colchester

Non-Speaking Roles

Many plays have characters that support idea through only their presence. 'Extras', as they are called, regularly appear holding shields and spears, or pass briefly across the stage, yet they are highly relevant to the play. The non-speaking role complements or contrasts with the ideas of situation, and they dress in accordance with these relationships.

In Ibsen's *Lady From The Sea*, the character Ballested guides a group of French and German tourists across the mountain paths of Norway. This select group of nineteenth-century travellers have arrived by steamer and some locals fear that tourism will spoil their little town. As extras, the travellers' costumes need to provide an insight into foreign custom and fashionable tastes abroad, and display attitudes to the changing times, notably the advent of tourism. Distinctive qualities and characteristics of the fabrics worn by the travellers will contrast with that of the local people.

5 VISION AND INTERPRETATION

THE DIRECTOR'S VISION

What the director thinks, sees and feels about the play is of the utmost importance. It is essential that you should take these ideas and impressions on board, exploring and developing them alongside your own. The issues the director wishes to raise or emphasize are vital points of reference for the designer, guiding and steering artistic interpretation.

The relationship of the audience to the acting space, and the configurations and

A stylized interior setting with realistic looking characters, made more dramatically intimate through the focus of lighting. Paul Daintry, Alastair Cording and Daniel Harcourt in Hansel and Gretel. *Director: Jonathan Holloway. Lighting: Ace McCarron. Lyric Theatre with Pop Up Theatre*

arrange-ments of actors within the acting area form an important part of the director's vision. Directors block actors into positions that establish focus and draw attention to the moment. The blocking becomes specific to the theatre space, set design and audience. The designer must be able to support the director's approach to handling structural relationships – how he intends to use the defined space, through blocking and movement, affects design. The spatial characteristics play up against and in support of the physical movements of character. These movements and the manner in which they are executed affect costume. The impact the director wishes a costume to have is dependant on the play's relationships.

INTERPRETATION

The process of interpretation begins with the director and designer doing research. A concept for a production can only be established when the play is well understood. The sense of direction is an interpretation, and this is naturally both objective and subjective. Interpretations are likely to vary, depending on the individuals involved. The team's sensibilities are reflected in the production's direction and design. Different productions of the same play may reflect fundamentally different interpretations.

The acting area is enlarged through lighting, and these Russian folklore-inspired characters broaden their own manner and gesture. The cast of Hansel and Gretel: *Paul Daintry, Sarah Stockbridge, Anna Savva, Daniel Harcourt. Director: Jonathan Holloway. Lighting: Ace McCarron. Lyric Theatre with Pop Up Theatre*

The director's contact with the actor is immediate and real, they form an intimate collaborative relationship. Directors control the rehearsal proceedings. They instruct, offer insight and advise. The role of the costume designer is to support the director's interpretation of character relationships, their discourse and action. Having ideas is a key part of realizing any work, but conviction and belief need to be guided by a practical and imaginative handling of the theatrical elements. These combine to form a harmonious, balanced design.

THE AUDIENCE AND TYPE OF THEATRE

Knowing your audience is important. However, fully anticipating what they will like or dislike is near impossible. Making predictions or assumptions on their behalf may prove to be a gamble. Theatres can attract quite different types of audience, depending on how they market

themselves, and to whom they target their plays. It is the artistic director's job to consider what type of audience the play should pitch itself at.

Appreciating how things have changed since a play was written may offer an insight to how it may be interpreted by modern audiences. Historical plays often seem relevent to contemporary issues in society. A play's content may entertain or stimulate one audience, but shock or repel another. It is up to the creative team to decide how the audience will interpret, understand and enjoy a play.

Styles of performance may suit a particular performing space. Venues generally fall into one of the following categories: arena stage; proscenium, or proscenium with apron extension; thrust stage; traverse stage; theatre-in-the-round; studio theatre; or site-specific locations which are generally not initially established as theatres. Productions within an alternative or site-specific space require additional research into establishing what the potential audience is likely to be and how they may be targetted.

Tip

As I began to see the actors in fittings and later in dress rehearsals I realized that, as a director, I had agreed to a concept that constricted the actors beyond the point of them being able to encompass it. Had we more time for the actors to gradually put the pieces on piece by piece and find some dialogue with the clothing, we might have been able to achieve the overall 'look' without it being a burden. The actors needed to have time to achieve that important relationship with the way they dressed, making a difference between an awkward production and an integrated one. Designers must read the play from the point of view of the actors. As a form of research, designers should experience the acting process...they should wear and play in what another designer designs.

Martha Henry

MICHAEL HALBERSTAM   BABE 3.

'KNIGHT OF THE BURNING PESTLE'

HORSE-PLAY

'KNIGHT OF THE BURNING PESTLE'

Making Adjustments On Tour

On tour, theatres and venues will inevitably vary in size, therefore touring productions may require a set to be altered, and actors will require additional rehearsals. Lighting is especially affected by touring. When there is likely to be variable lighting, aspects of costume breakdown or ageing need to be carefully considered. Heavy breakdown of costume, when brightly lit, may appear as only a treatment rather than an illusion. Space is also at a premium when touring: the proposed transport will act as an additional constraint for design. Small and medium-scale touring limitations are the starting points of design discussions. Costume maintenance may be restricted to under-garments or garments which can be washed. Outer layers need be sympathetic to the problem. Weight and portability is another issue.

Drawings which show the process for working through an idea to find the most appropriate design to complement character.
Knight of the Burning Pestle.
Stratford Festival Theatre

APPROACHING THE PLAY

The play, as it reads on the page, seems a lifeless matter and it is the task of the director and designer to create the vision for staging the play. This vision is an interpretation, which is all about telling the story and clarifying the playwright's intentions. The creative team serve to support the ever-changing stage focus through making that which is significant clear and articulate. The actors lift the play on to its feet and through performance give it life.

Prior to reading the play, study the back cover and the forwarding pages. Look for notes about the play and playwright along with its date. Read any translator or editor notes.. This information is useful as it provides an initial impression of the play.

Publications

The play may be found in different publications, and each may read a little differently, especially if the play is translated from a foreign language. Publications may coincide with a particular staged production. Check to see if the publication is for the playwright's original production. When you are asked to read a play, be clear which publication your director is reading or wishing you to read.

Copyright

There are laws which protect the language, and, in some cases, the staging of the play. When passages are cut from plays it is to keep within the laws of copyright. Actors throughout the rehearsal period are reminded

Rafe and his trusty steed with Squire Tim.
Michael Halberstam and Geoff McBride.
Knight of the Burning Pestle.
Directors: Bernard Hopkins and Pat Galloway.
Lighting: Kevin Fraser. Stratford Festival Theatre.
Courtesy of the Stratford Festival Archives

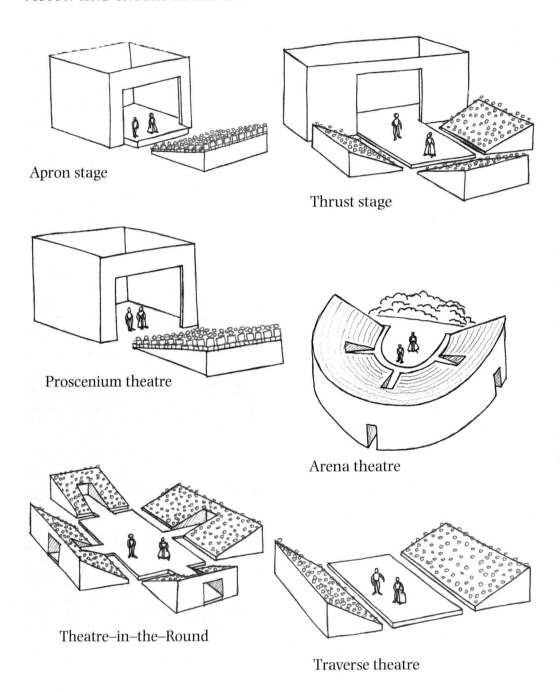

Apron stage

Thrust stage

Proscenium theatre

Arena theatre

Theatre–in–the–Round

Traverse theatre

Arena stage. Proscenium theatre. Proscenium theatre with apron extension. Traverse theatre.
Thrust stage. Theatre-in-the-round.

The cast in rehearsal with the monster head of Grendel, and later with monster head and hands of Grendel. Walter James, Milenka Marosh, Andrew Mallett, David Roecliffe, Nancy McClean, Paul Ryan. Director: Roman Stefanski. Beowulf. Polka Theatre

White card model, showing the proposed layout for doors and rooms off. **Dial M For Murder.**
Grand Theatre

to use the exact wording and phrasing, as the playwright intended.

Stage Directions

Publications which coincide with a production frequently include their own stage directions, which may not be those specified by the playwright. Such directions appear between the dialogue, either in italic or in parentheses. When stage directions are not of the author's hand, it should be a considered issue as to whether you use them or not. Stage directions describe the character's action, and they often describe props being used. They are not part of a character's speech.

Set Descriptions

Architectural layout described or suggested by the playwright is of particular interest. A set description, described by a publication for a production which did not involve the playwright, should be overlooked. The architectural or spatial positions that offer entrance and exit, are critically important. Where exits lead off to, and what is suggested beyond, matters quite considerably. In a thriller, like Dial M for Murder by Frederick Knot, the logic of the architectural layout is fundamental to the action. Here the positioning of the main door, to the garden door, to the bedroom door is crucial.

Acts and Scenes

1. Scan through the play and read the introduction to each act and scene.
2. List each act and scene by its appropriate number.
3. Note location, specific date, time, and season.
4. Ascertain whether each location is a private or public property, and note the landlord particulars.
5. Note the details of architectural layout, such as doors and windows.
6. List the characters that appear within each scene.
7. Note the position of the intended interval or intermission.
8. Consider the duration of the acts and scenes.

Act, Scene Page	Actor/ Charac	Run Time	Exit	Change	Ent	Time	Loc	Notes
3.1.45	MISS COLLINS/ MARGOT	39m	SL	- Wig	SL	35m	DRSS Room	2nd Interval N.B - needs to re-ent w/purse and coat
3.1.45	Mr Ziegler/ Max	39m	SR	- dark khaki trousers - orange sweater + blk sweater + green cords	SL	17m	DRSS Room	2nd interval keeps on jacket
3.1.45	Mr Schurmann/ Tony max	39m	SL	- grey tweed trousers - brown cardigan - straight tie + brown tweed trousers + beige knit vest + brown tie + grey tweed sports jckt + raincoat + brown hat	SL	15m	DRSS Room	2nd interval
3.1.45	Mr Hopkins/ Hubbard	39m	SL	+ raincoat	SL	22m	DRSS Room	2nd interval carries it only
3.1.47	Mr Schurmann/ Tony	15s	-	- brown hat - raincoat	-	-	on stg	Left on hall chair +hooks
3.1.51	Mr Hopkins/ Hubbard	7m	-	- hat - raincoat	-	-	on stg	Oncoat hooks on coat hooks
3.1.57	Mr Hopkins/ Hubbard	17m	-	+ hat	-	-		Hubbard strikes Tony's raincoat Left Re-enters with it
3.1.58	Mr Schurmann/ Tony	18m	SL					Strikes Hubbard rain-coat L Re-enters with it

A page from the plot for change of costumes throughout the play, timings and positions for the changes are included. Dial M for Murder. Grand Theatre

Singers Nicholas Ransley and Lorenzo Carola sharing the same role on alternate nights, in discussion with the director Thomas de Mallet Burgess on the set for Albert Herring. Guildhall School of Music and Drama

THE CHARACTERS

Character List

Note:

1. The characters and their names, ages, and nationalities. The internal relationships such as blood relations, positions of rank and power, marriage, allies, friends and foes.
2. The social class orders such as kings, court nobles, aristocracy, merchants, professionals, traders, peasants and beggars.
3. The roles that double or triple (some plays require the actor to play several roles).

Doubling Roles

Doubling may become necessary for financial reasons. When actors take on two roles, they enter into two characters, therefore costume, make-up and wigs need pay particular attention to supporting the differences, especially when timings of exit and entrance are tight. Some quick-changes demand that costume changes be kept to a minimum. Anticipating quick-change timings, and what can be achieved as a change is important in design. Once into rehearsals realistic timings will be given.

The Large Cast

A long and involved character list inevitably poses questions as to how best to allocate the budget. Any rough costing, which is to be encouraged at an early stage, will involve thinking through the approach most appropriate for the production. Being practical does not mean one becomes less creative. On the contrary, it should encourage innovation.

The character list for J M Barrie's Peter Pan is quite extensive. It includes a mother, father and children; magical characters like Peter Pan and Tinkerbell; Nana the household dog; native Indians; pirates; a crocodile and a variety of other animals; a large family of lost boys; and mermaids. Early attempts to cost out and balance the budget will help to establish an appropriate concept for staging it. This then gives the set and costume designer a constraint to work within, all before one sets the artistic pencil to paper.

6 READING THE PLAY

Plays often take many hours to read thoroughly, so be sure to set aside an appropriate amount of time. Complex plots and involved character relationships may make the read-through hard going, so make it all the easier by being comfortable, and avoid unnecessary interruptions.

Appreciate that plays take months, even years to write. When you have the opportunity to design a new play, the playwright may be in residence, and how you interpret visually will be vitally important to them.

A play may challenge both your emotions and intellect. How you react to the first read is important. Set out to enjoy it, or at least find it an adventure. Allow it to make an impression on you. The first read should simply be for general understanding. Subsequent read throughs for breakdown and analysis, and the full understanding of the play comes with time and further investigation. Characters and their relationships, along with the play's structure, can be beguiling, evasive and ethereal.

After the first read, take account of your impressions. Ask first what you think the play is saying, then how you feel character supports this. What the play has to say to you matters considerably, and your initial impressions must be put down on paper. Impressions should be caught while still fresh in the mind. Sketch and take notes after reading each act. Initial impressions may be unclear, let this come through in what you put down. The more impressions you gather, the more they will add up to something. Have confidence in your impressions and avoid thinking too literally about the characters, place and situation at this stage.

Analysis and research take time. Investigations into the play should be in stages or steps. Structure; character and character relationships; social, political and economic issues; period details relating to time, place, location and situation; mood and atmosphere, all need to be investigated. Then there is the charting of characters coming and going within scenes, what they should be wearing, and how timings affect changes. With each of these investigations,

A student's painterly impression for scene interpretation.
Dali-Costume design at Central St Martins

A student creating an impression of
characters within a colour field,
interpretations of a scene.
Dali-Costume design at Central St Martins

the designer must always be aware of the effect each may have on the play as a whole.

Set and costume design takes weeks, frequently months, yet there never seems enough time. Planning a schedule will help to set an order of things to be done. The process of design is a lot about problem solving. Time for reflection is also needed in order to look at things afresh. Solutions come about slowly, often only becoming apparent once a considerable amount of work has been done.

CAPTURING FIRST IMPRESSIONS

Drawing, painting and collage offer a wealth of method and technique for expression. Equip your studio with a selection from this list:

- Size A3 and A4 college cartridge paper, lightweight and heavy
- Soft and hard pencils from 2H–6B
- Coloured pencils, crayons, chalks and pastels
- Charcoal, watercolour or gouache paints
- Coloured inks
- Craft glue
- Scissors
- An assortment of magazines (preferably with a matt surface to the pages) and newspapers
- Coloured tissue paper

Exercise
After the first read through, create an impression that captures the overall mood of each scene. Work boldly and allow for abstraction. Avoid pushing the play into a shape at this stage, and let your feelings guide you instead. Whilst a naive image is as welcome as an expressionistic one, steer away from drawing people and figures at this point. The play may seem to say something specific straight away – allow this to find a form through your drawing or collage. Pattern and texture may feature in your impression, if its characteristics are coarse, jagged, or heavily pitted then let surface texture appear on the page. Colours may be predominant, perhaps dripping contrasting colour on a wet page establishes mingling relationships which complement your impressions. Think in terms of making a mark on the page using line, texture, shade, colour and pattern which equate to such words as aggression, passion, cowardice, panic, fear, sadness and desperation. Handle the medium in such a way that it says something particular. A light-hearted feeling may often be described through spontaneous or determined fine pencil or ink lines and the use of pastel shades. Use stark contrast and shadow play to add mystery and suspense. Marks can express nervous energy, sedate manners, sloppiness and anarchy. Use the whole of the page, and aim to cover the white of the page until any white remaining is intended to be there. Impressions should be labelled with the act or scene number.

A student collage for characters within a setting, scene interpretation.
Dali-Costume design at Central St Martins

Allow interpretations to take you into the animal and vegetable kingdoms, where comparisons can make for exciting relationships and enable you to observe a situation from another perspective.

Exercise
Consider the external forces that shape and influence a situation. First, establish whether a situation is domestic, national, international or global. Ask if the influences and situation are particular to any one time and place, or whether they may be seen in another form or context, and consider what this may be. Through this you will gain a more meaningful insight into, and deeper understanding of, the play. The influences that shape situation can be the focus for the next step.

Take some A3 size pages of college cartridge. Choose several principal characters or any that stand out within a scene. Create interpretations of the characters and their relationships to others. Consider first the dynamics between characters. Focus on tensions and bonds, consider their contrasts and harmonies. Avoid too figurative an image, instead work loosely and boldly with collage or paint. Work characters together, alongside one another or in various groupings. Let dynamics be the focus, this enables impressionistic or abstract qualities to prevail.

Exercise
For this drawing exercise use charcoal, a soft 3B–6B pencil, chalk or pastel. Place the point on the page then close your eyes. Think of two characters and a situation or moment in the play involving them both. Their mass and volume will differ, perhaps they play against one another, each making the other look different. Without removing the instrument from the page, draw out the impression. Think of the character without clothing. Here the emphasis is on shape. Avoid looking for details or features, capture an impression. Do this for all characters in the scene. Explore weight and pressure which produces soft and hard, light and dark contrasts.

Exercise

Use one continuous line, where the pencil or pen point never comes off the page, to explore characters' shapes in space. Draw one shape connecting to another, be it human or object. Let the foreground and background mingle. Close your eyes and try to see a scene, then with eyes still closed, draw it out, keeping all things linked. This way character and location become inextricably linked, as they are in plays.

Script Analysis

Who

- are the characters? List them all, together with their appropriate titles.
- are the associates, friends, family and foes of each character?
- are the protagonists, antagonists, leading actors, supporting roles, non-speaking roles and chorus?
- appears in each scene? Make a chart showing the scene breakdown.
- doubles or triples their parts?

What

- does each character stands for? Note their ideals and aspirations, and their role in the play's action.
- social classes do the characters come from? Classify them into hierarchies and social orders.
- differences stand out between the characters' political, social and economic views?
- is the play saying scene by scene? Encapsulate in a few words.
- type or within what genre would you classify the play?
- makes the characters 'tick', what thoughts motivate them into action?
- traits does each character have? Make a list.
- do you think was happening prior to the play beginning, and what is likely to happen afterwards?

A student's continuous line drawing, for developing character.
Drawn with the eyes closed. Salvo Manciagli.
Dali-Costume design at Central St Martins

- are the outside influences which shape the play?
- highlights or moments of importance seem significant for moving the play forward?
- effect has the play had on you?
- is the role of structure in making the play work?

A student's painted impression of characters.
Anna Strobl. Dali-Costume design at Central St Martins

Where

- geographically and culturally does the action takes place?
- are the entrances and exits for each actor?
- do actors come from and go to, beyond the confines of setting?

When

- do the scenes take place? List the time, day, month, season, year, and differences between the scenes.
- did the play have its greatest impact on the audience? Note the range of reactions.
- do the characters stand to lose or gain the most, and by what means?

Why

- do the play's events and situations happen?
- has the playwright chosen this subject and employed these characters?
- do the characters affect one another, and why do they come together?
- are the characters introduced in such a sequence, and why has the play been structured in this way?
- should the play be staged before a modern audience?
- might issues be considered confrontational, provoking, harmless or old fashioned?

7 HISTORICAL RESEARCH

DEFINING 'PERIOD'

Statements that concern themselves with people, place and time, need supporting with period accuracy, and the dates that define period are essential to any discussion on history. Dates, however, are more in keeping with fact. Reference to period can tend to make homogeneous the people, their ideas and ideals. Such generalizations can be both misleading and an unfair judgement of the times.

There will often be marked contrasts between the beginning and end of a period, which should not be considered as having boundaries fixed by dates, for there are evolving characteristics which make start and cut-off points difficult to establish.

Dates offer, to the student, vivid pictures of social, economic and political climate.

A fine pen and ink character drawing for Hector, showing period dress as comfortable and easy to wear. Useful notes accompany Brian Jackson's design for Swan Song. Stratford Festival Theatre

Tip
Every play seems to have its 'period'. Character in period dress is helped enormously. It is usually more difficult for us to imagine the outward personification of the character in a period costume, therefore the costume usually takes on proportionally more importance, whether it's helpful or a hindrance. You can be just as put off by an ill-suited modern costume as by a badly made or conceived period one. Even in a modern play one very seldom is wearing precisely what one would wear at home, nor would one wish to. There is always an element of 'coming to' the costume, and it to you.
Martha Henry

A remarkably likeable and delightful character, full of intriguing detail from head to toe. Tattle in Love For Love.
Designer: Ann Curtis. Stratford Festival Theatre

Reference to dates when discussing playwrights and their works can prove to be both enlightening and informative. The aspects of period, which we as researchers should find of interest, are those conditions of change which appear to shape a people, place and time. The influences that affect ideals and attitudes are of great significance. The impact of historical orders and systems may still be observed many hundreds of years after their first appearance.

Establishing the playwright's proposed dates, and placing the play in its correct historical context encourages factual discussion. This leads to a strengthening of the bond between creative interpretations and the playwright's aim.

RESOURCES FOR HISTORICAL RESEARCH

A wide range of books and encyclopaedias on costume are available. There are specialist pattern books; publications from costume exhibitions; reference books on fashion designers and fashion houses; books on underwear, ties, shoes, hats, spectacles, hair and so on. Having your own collection of books and reference material is invaluable. Be particular about having books that source and date the image. General dates are of less value than specific ones. With reference books on period cut and tailoring, the designer can better date an image.

The fine arts are the richest source for historical reference. National museums and galleries such as the V&A and The National Portrait Gallery offer collections of remarkable interest to the costume designer. Drawings and paintings, as much as sculptures, cameos, miniatures, illuminations and illustrations offer valuable information. Fashion plates and patterns prove highly informative. Photography's candid nature makes it a superb source of information about people, time and place. Costume collections further inform the designer on construction and material.

Libraries
Main libraries have useful reference sections where the books are guaranteed to be on the shelf. Specialist bookshops offer old collectibles, which will often include engravings and colour plates of interest. Second-hand bookshops are always worth checking out. Most reputable bookshops have theatre, drama and fashion sections. Theatre bookshops offer collections of plays and reference books on theatre craft.

Paintings and Sculpture
Early period research will have you looking at illuminated manuscripts, painted murals,

frescos, brass rubbings and tomb effigies. The knight and his damsel lie in wait, they exhibit fascinating aspects of period dress. Visit your local crypt, church and cathedral to see such remarkably interesting effigies.

The works of well-known artists are accessible and can prove a great source of inspiration. Characters in plays, however, are often more ordinary than the people portrayed by celebrated artists. Local artists and those simply less internationally celebrated frequently offer a more intimate, even domestic insight, which is sometimes overlooked by the more famous artists. They may be harder to track down, yet it is worth the hunt. Galleries are a starting point, look at the collection of past exhibition catalogues. These artists may have exhibited in a group show rather than solo. The cultural departments of some embassies or consulates may have useful information on artists of a particular country

NO. 3. OUTDOOR MORNING COSTUME.

Fashion Plates

Fashion plates do not generally reflect the appearance of most ordinary people, although they frequently wear a modified version of what fashion plates portray.

It is useful to look at fashion plates from previous years. Current trends are often an update of previous ones. Some plays ooze style, and the designer will enjoy interpreting and adapting fashion plates into real clothing. Fashion plates show off unobtainable waists and bust lines. The distortion exaggerates height. The actor is rarely of such ideal proportions, thus making any fashion plate a design which clearly needs re-thinking to fit and complement the actor's proportions.

Photography

The portable camera brought photography to the masses. From 1840 onwards photography has served to enlighten us on all aspects of life with pictures capturing the nation at work

NO. 4. AFTERNOON CARRIAGE COSTUME.

Fashion plates from The Queen, *The Lady's Newspaper of 1880.*

Rural working men and boys. An informative photograph found in a secondhand shop.

and play. Like the artist, the photographer has control over the image. The subject and the arrangements of its parts is open to manipulation and interpretation. Advances in digital photography and computer graphics have led to great advances in controlling and manipulating the image. Photography can be an enormous help to the designer and knowing something about the photographer and his methods can be enlightening.

Costume Collections

Institutes of costume and fashion conduct research, collect for reference and exhibit. Their exhibitions are often accompanied by useful catalogues and publications. The collection may be made available for study purposes and their libraries may be open to

Note

Photographs of Victorian domestic staff, in some cases, reveal a desire to emulate their employer's dress sense. This taking on the guise of another, while actually retaining an inferior social class position, features in many plays. Late nineteenth-century senior staff members, those who had served long terms with one household, might have found themselves in elevated positions upon retiring. This deserved status would allow them to mingle freely and hold conversations with the employer's guests.

view upon request. Such institutes regularly offer lectures and talks on the history of costume. Museums may have a costume department, with archives of specialist interest. The museum library may also prove a very useful resource.

Due to the vulnerable nature of fabrics, dyes and prints, collections of historical costume safeguard their treasures by not exhibiting them frequently, unless the conditions for exhibit are under strict control. Fabric's natural enemies are moths, household pests, sun and bright light, moisture and sweat. Costume collections are kept boxed in controlled atmospheres. Natural fibres age, they become fragile though wear and tear and they suffer from exposure to the natural elements, especially light. Working-class dress as well clothing for the middle classes simply wore out over time. The examples we see on exhibit have been carefully preserved. Court dress has every chance of surviving, unless it is damaged through water or fire. The costume designer should take every opportunity to observe real period garments. Portraits, fashion plates and photographs rarely show the front, side and rear views comprehensively.

Films
Documentary films can prove valuable for period research. Hollywood movies and period films are of less interest as they tend to show designed interpretations. Films shot in contemporary dress may prove more useful in gauging the general feel of a period. Few films show the real person on the street.

Trade, Guild and Craft Institutes
Trade, guild and craft institutes and associations house historical archives which offer a great resource for researching occupational dress. Local libraries are a valuable source of information about local traders, guilds and manufacturers – their photo archives are often surprisingly comprehensive. Most libraries sell local history publications.

Uniforms, trade apparel and occupational dress has evolved and tradition plays an important role. Occupational dress shows regional variety, with the look dependent on the geographical area and local textile manufacture. The growth of industry and new skills acquired has led to radical change in trade dress and uniform.

Books of Etiquette
Handbooks on etiquette can prove an invaluable aid to understanding historical modes and manners. They quite clearly define tradition and custom for the time, and offer an insight into contemporary attitudes towards gender.

The Pocket Book of Etiquette, published in 1956 (see Bibliography), offers guidance on matters of manners, custom and dress for social occasions such as parties, travel, proposals and visits; together with advice on professional business matters; treatment of employees and announcements of all kinds. For example:

Smoking: Women should never smoke in any street. Men should never smoke when out walking in the street with a lady.

Mourning: Members of the bereaved household should wear black until about two weeks after the funeral. Thereafter they wear subdued colours for another two weeks. Long periods of mourning are no longer necessary.

Meeting in the street: A lady does not recognize any gentleman until he has raised his hat to her. A gentleman is expected to raise his hat on entering and leaving any shop, on joining or leaving any table outside a cafe, on entering and leaving any occupied rail coach or aircraft. It is not necessary to stand head uncovered when talking to a lady

A playful contrast of styles for characters of a commedia dell'arte *type, in the musical* **Mascarade.** *Mikado Company*

in the open, however when under cover the hat remains off.

Gloves: A lady is not expected to remove a glove when shaking hands, however to express more friendship she may wish to remove it.

Walking: When two ladies walk with a gentleman they do not walk with him between them, the most senior lady shall take the side of the gentleman.

Casual clothing: A man should avoid casual forms of dress for serious work, for even though management may not pass comment to him directly, the impression to his firm and clients may sooner or later tell against him

At the theatre: A gentlemen should remove hat, coat, gloves and not take them into the auditorium of a concert hall, theatre or opera house. This is only permitted at the cinema.

HISTORICAL AUTHENTICITY

Research into the origins of fashion and period dress is a fascinating study. The influences that affect fashion, its modes and manners, is most enlightening. Clothes both evolve and take dramatic turns in direction due to social, economic, or political reasons.

Acquiring a knowledge of period dress places the costume designer at a great advantage. Historical cut and detail may then be employed on practical terms, with the designer having a more objective eye. An appreciation of differing periods, which appear to exhibit fundamental similarities, socially or politically may make it easier to consider shifting or updating a play.

Plays rarely stand as either historically accurate or as a social documentary. The playwright may explore the truth of events, but the play will encompass much more than historically accurate fact. The interpretation of character, relationship and event is a manipulation intended for dramatic effect. Too much attention to historical accuracy in costuming may take the character into a reality which is at odds with the actor's performance and the convention of theatre.

An actor's physical shape may not resemble that of the role he is supposed to be playing and they may be greatly diminished or overwhelmed by period costume. This can convey entirely the wrong impression, perhaps making a king appear comical rather than regal. Audience expectations can often be rather one dimensional, based on popular images. It must be the aim of the designer to create a costume appropriate to the period, which will enable the actor to achieve the anticipated presence through stature, poise and manner.

All design elements must work in harmony to achieve a measure of overall authenticity. Properties accompanying period costume require the same attention to detail as designs for location, setting and lighting. It is usually a question of balance, of deciding how much additional information is needed to support character in location. A simple, bold setting often proves successful.

Overall proportions are of particular concern on-stage. The stage configuration plays an important part on determining the scale for shape and detail. The further away the audience, the less finery shows itself off.

ERA AND EPOCH

The characters in plays belong to an age within which each has a relationship to a particular era or decade, which show variations in attitude, style and manner. Our grandparents have shown us how preferences for fashion tend to hang on in society. It is natural that with differences in age, characters will display something of the past, present and future. Some individuals, of course, will reject contemporary styles.

GEOGRAPHY AND CUSTOM

The weave, pattern and decoration of textiles have historical and geographical significance. The location in which scenes are set may often be defined through material and decoration. Custom, tradition and ritual are unique to people and place. There are even regional differences for the same occasion or event. Cultures develop their own unique forms of symbolism for status. Global images relating to state celebration are extraordinarily varied.

Each country has their own image for justice, honour, service, office, rank and order.

Superstition is often an important cultural influence. Culture fends off and keeps at bay, evil, through ritual. Fear is a frequently explored subject in plays. Understanding societies' fears should enlighten the designer researching a play's period.

There is considerable superstition surrounding colour. Culture attaches significance to colour, and it becomes symbolic through custom and tradition. There are ceremonies and rituals that are shared across nations yet the details of each are different due to traditional beliefs and

An excessive proportion which would belittle any head. The Queen, *The Lady's Newspaper*

Design leaning on the primitive, to support the ritual of **The Rite Of Spring.**
Las Vegas Civic Ballet

superstitions – in the Far East, for example, red is for weddings and white for death.

HEIRARCHY IN DRESS

Fashion has a degree of political relevance. Power is often exhibited through a uniformed image. Throughout history, proportioning, cut and fabric have distinguished hierarchy, rank and the ruling classes. Fashion has also been used to highlight differences in ideals in politics.

Costume design must reflect social class and rank by first appreciating how important the differences are in context to the play's structure. If the direct discourse does not spell it out, the tone of the work might. Modes of language can offer some measure of hierarchy and class. Design needs to question whether what the audience hears is enough to support these differences. By adding degrees of suggested contrast, the interplay begins. Often, small touches in costuming can effectively communicate these differences. When developing the characters, work on them together and see them set against one another.

Uniformity

Corporations impose rules of dress and codes of behaviour on members and employees. It is a form of protection through a uniformity of image, values and standards. The image is seen to be all important, and what it represents or symbolises needs protecting. Uniformity takes away a measure of individuality. Through corporate identity, the only individual feature that stands out is the face, as hairstyle, make-up and decoration with jewellery will also have their limitations. Uniform draws attention to itself, therefore affecting the outsider. Uniformity may give the impression that all those taking part are equal, and contact with one will be like contact with any one of the others, including the 'top dog'.

Established faiths and collectives be they political, religious, or social, frequently display a uniformity in their dress. Their members wear a uniform, which makes them often internationally recognizable. A spin-off from the main group may show signs of adapting their image to their territory. Some groups re-establish older customs and traditions and find renewed strengths of solidarity.

RADICALISM IN FASHION

At times, fashion trends have caused waves of alarm. Society tends to establish boundaries for fashion, and differing rules and codes of

74

dress are observed worldwide. Fashions that appear suitable in one country may be inappropriate elsewhere. Religion and belief has its influence upon dress in society. Taboo lies on the fringes of society, yet it is often clearly defined.

Some culture shocks reverberate through society and quickly fade, others are outlawed. Throughout history, the church and political courts have legislated against fashionable trends. Research reveals that Acts of Parliament set down laws against fashion trends and excess. The Renaissance shirt was considered an undergarment, and therefore was thought to have sexual and alluring characteristics. The Italians lowered the male neckline, with a horizontal cut shirt front. The doublet was cut lower still to draw the eye to the suggestive underwear and revealed chest. By the sixteenth century, the shirt front showed an excess of cut and style, and soon came under the controlling hand of state law.

Extremes frequently become part of the establishment at a later date, after the shock has subsided, and society sees it as less of a threat. Moral and ethical groups sound alarm bells to ward off such evil, yet liberal-minded people see change as inevitable and have less real fear of it. The ideology that is attached to a radical look is frequently more threatening then the look itself. The punk and skinhead images have both over time become integrated into acceptable streetwear.

Fashion scandals may be linked to anti-fashion movements, which aim to reform standards of dress. The Reform-Dress movement of the late 1800s, for example, initiated an anti-corset campaign which carried on well into the first quarter of the 1900s.

Non-conformists

Like the radical, the non-conformist can cause unsettling reactions. Characters on-stage are continually reacting to one another, and how

The cadet Orsino with informative and interesting detailed views for the front, the back, sword belt, side of breeches and cap. Twelfth Night. *Designer: Ann Curtis. Stratford Festival Theatre*

they dress has some impact on that reaction. Appearances frequently cause adverse reactions – people can stand out because of their appearance. They may have no interest in or concern for fashion. They may be clean yet appear unkempt, sloppy, even slovenly. They may hang on to old habits and old outfits, believing them still to have some practical value.

Resisting change proves hard work. People rise up to resist it, yet change is a part of the fabric of life. Characters expressing individual values that are in marked contrast to other characters' values, may well become apparent through the design.

Design can highlight these differences. They can be made theatrical through concentrating on the associations that link values in society, values that can be seen in the attitudes of dress which groups choose to adopt.

THE MODERN DRESS PRODUCTION

Modern dress is a term for costume from our own time. An audience finds it easy to identify with modern dress on-stage. Because it is so accessible, it is easier to recognize ourselves and others in the characters we observe. We all have a well-developed appreciation of contemporary beauty and aesthetic values derived through our experiences, and feel comfortable with the dress of our time, that of our parents and possibly our grandparents. Whilst contemporary modes of dress may liberate the production from unnecessary period detail, updating other aspects of the play may prove to be more of a challenge.

A historical play may be updated, but it remains a period piece. Whilst some plays sit well within a later period, the reasons for updating and modernizing must be seriously considered as it can be a complex process. Research both periods thoroughly, look for tangible social or political parallels that relate to the play. Adding a sense of the contemporary to, 'how things were', moves events forward into more familiar territory.

Present day traditions, ceremonies, pageants and occasions can all influence design when updating and modernizing a play, and audience expectations must enter into the equation. There will also be variations between past and present notions of good taste, romance, allure, style and so on ,which design must reflect.

MEN'S CLOTHING

Constraints

A certain measure of shape in costume relates to attitudes concerning sex appeal and attraction. Shape through tailoring and decoration can create allure. The viewer's eye is constantly moving over and around the figure and the emphasis is often quite clearly meant to take the eye away from or draw it towards that which is significant, in terms of allure.

Historically, men's dress has often appeared freer of the constraints imposed upon the female form. Nonetheless, fighting whilst in armour, in pumpkin hose and doublet, or in heavily tailored multi-layered uniforms, seems today to be both impractical and restrictive.

Squire Tim. Pen and ink rendering.
Knight of the Burning Pestle

The slashing of costumes in the 1500s originated with men at war wishing to release themselves from the constraints of period style. A German emperor of the sixteenth century allowed his soldiers to slash their garments so as to increase comfort. There are extreme examples of tailored slashing in the 'Plunderhose' of the 1500s. These baggy breeches were elaborately constructed, comprising three layers – the inner lining which fitted the leg and retained the outer shape; the outer layer which may have been constructed in slashed panels; and the baggy or gathered inner middle layer which showed through the slashing as contrast. The outer fabric might have been of leather, velvet or silk. The slashing displayed a patterned overall design. Through the slashing one saw finely gathered lightweight silk. The inner lining may have had between forty and one hundred yards of gathered silk. The silhouette showed off the thigh and posterior.

Breeches

Breeches of this period often find their way on to the stage. They are, however, an expensive design to realize. Their very complicated nature demands some compromise. The breeches are part of an ensemble, a total look. They were worn with elaborately padded and slashed doublets with full sleeves in the same design. Shoes were also slashed in the same manner, revealing inner layers.

Trousers

At the end of the eighteenth century all men wore breeches except sailors and shepherds, who wore long trousers. In 1807, the young Prince of Wales may have helped establish a trend by wearing long white sailor's trousers on holiday in Brighton. However, it was not until the 1830s that trousers became socially acceptable.

The Suit, Shirt and Vest

With the exception of work in heavy foundries, men remained well buttoned-up throughout the Victorian and Edwardian eras. In fact, the British working classes wore a suit with waistcoat up to about 1945. A collar and tie was standard dress for all working-class men, both in and out of doors, throughout this period. The jacket was the first item to be eventually discarded, leaving the waistcoat, shirt, collar and tie to become a popular common look. Eventually the waistcoat and tie were removed, giving over to braces or suspenders and shirt.

Until the 1920s the undervest, an undergarment handed down from the Victorians, was always sleeved. Around this period however, it evolved into the singlet, and soon after one begins to see it suggestively revealed through a partially unbuttoned shirt front. During the last quarter of the twentieth century, we see it becoming an overgarment. The roots of this simple garment can be traced back some 800 years from its earliest origins as a cotton shift worn as an overgarment, then to become an undergarment, to again become an overgarment. Today, the singlet features in a wide range of colours, knits, patterns and materials – a popular casual garment for healthy working men and women.

WOMEN'S CLOTHING

The dramatic political and economic impact of the French Revolution led to a great reformation in dress, led on by the English. The Napoleonic Wars of 1793–1814 turned the face of fashion back towards classical times. The silhouette was streamlined through shedding heavy, structured underclothes and adopting a lightweight mode of dress which allowed the body freedom of movement and breathability. The attitudes associated with previous times of prudery gave way to accepting the look, with its lack of underclothes, as being neither overly erotic nor having any great class distinction. Clothing had suddenly become more comfortable and practical.

Later the prudery of Victorian society led to extreme measures being taken to ensure the female form should again be appropriately covered. The Victorians created taboos for the whole of the female body. The enlarged silhouettes in the skirts served to remove from the wearer any suggestion of eroticism. However, the movement of the hooped skirt proved to be a strong erotic attraction, as was the bustle. The emphasis on the posterior and the hips retained men's interest until the early 1900s when the fashion began to wane.

By the First World War, women were seen to wear trousers, prior to this they had only been worn while they worked in the mines.

Constraints

Shape demands the underpinnings be rigidly structured. Without a contrived foundation in underclothes, fashion has only the figure to cling to. Only a few times throughout history do we see simple, body-clinging fabric dresses. Underpinnings in the shape of corsets, hooped skirts, bustles, hip and bum rolls add the necessary frame for fashion.

Women have suffered dramatically through fashion dictates – indeed some constraints proved not only uncomfortable but life-threatening. Whale-boned corsets crushed internal organs and made breathing difficult, toxic make-ups and hair dyes invited skin reactions, the weight and bulk over steel-hooped skirts put women at a great disadvantage when negotiating the streets. Eighteenth-century hairstyles reached ridiculous heights and were decked with all manner of inspired scenes from garden landscapes to sailing ships. The wearer would have experienced a great deal of difficulty in sleeping and by day the neck would have

suffered considerably. Heat was an additional problem, especially in the summer months. Life at the Seaside painted by W P Frith RA in 1854, shows women in full attire – boots and shoes, petticoats and overdress, long sleeves with gloves, hair fashionably styled, and the body further wrapped in shawls and scarves

UNDERCLOTHES AND UNDERWEAR

The earliest periods of outer dress, which were simple shift garments, later evolved into the underclothes or our basic underwear. With the shift being eventually covered over, these newly formed garments required altering to conform to the shape of the body. The shapes they began to take affected the shaped development of outer garments. This can be seen through to the twentieth century. From the corseted bustier to the bra, fashion has creatively shaped itself over and around the undergarment shape. Period silhouette has undergone amazing transformations, and the causes are intricately woven into the web of social, geographical, political, and economic climates of people and place.

Historically the working classes tended to dress in a more practical manner. Women, being less active, suffered from the cold much more than men. Right through to the eighteenth century, legs were kept almost totally covered and well concealed from men. Beneath their skirts, women did not cover their legs and thighs until well into the nineteenth century. From the Middle Ages women have fought off the cold by building up layers with wool petticoats and additional layered overskirts. Leather was the only alternative to wool for keeping warm, but this was always most predominant amongst working men rather than in fashionable wear. Women, however, forsook the warmer fabrics above the waist to retain their slender silhouette. Men generally have showed less fear or reserve in adding bulk to the torso by layering. Under the female bodice was worn a chemise made of cambric or linen in the upper classes and of cotton in working and lower classes. Both materials had the practical advantages of breathability and ease of cleaning.

Health and Hygiene

Health and hygiene did not take a hold on fashion, in the sense of fashionable underclothes, until less then two hundred years ago. It has since gone through remarkable changes. Cleanliness would not become an issue, until nearly the end of the eighteenth century. The 'Macaroni' of the 1770s established some precedent for general social cleanliness. This new social concern encouraged the individual to attend to keeping

the body, its underclothing and subsequent layers, immaculately clean. This reformation in hygiene was reinstating standards which had fallen by the wayside since the Roman times.

The Victorian era led to another reformation in cleanliness of underclothes and dress. The period is rich with new designs in undergarments for the purpose of concealing and cleanliness. The Edwardian period relaxed this excessive buttoned up silhouette, yet they also carried on pushing reforms in hygiene.

Victorian girls were taught to distrust and shy away from men wearing perfume. Scent was said to disguise. To hide a man's true odour, a most natural side-effect of hard work, was deemed suspicious. Body odour was acceptable, not considered offensive in the middle classes, and a gentleman without it was to be looked upon as having something to hide.

Materials of natural fibre complement location and setting. Tony Casement, Janet Bamford and Sally Mates in Starlight Cloak.
Director: Vicky Ireland. Lighting Neil Fraser. Polka Theatre. Photo: Roger Howard

Neat and tidy family values in **The Railway Children.**
Director: Michael Winter. Lighting: Jim Bowman. Setting: Vikie Le Sache. Mercury Theatre

By the time of the First World War it had become a common belief in society that all clothing should be protected through the wearing of differing forms of underwear. By 1920, the underwear industry had become a major commercial enterprise, and catalogues from the period show a remarkable range of items offering tremendous choice.

8   CREATING PERIOD DRESS

History is abundant with contrasting tastes, styles and manners. Attitude is reflected in silhouette, in the tailored cut, the material and its decoration. Playwrights incorporate contrasts of style, manner and behaviour traits into character. Such individual characteristics support the play's structure and dynamics.

When actors fail to achieve the attitude that moves character forward, design must reassess its contribution. One looks first to the foundations, then at restrictions caused by shape, fabric and the resulting movement. It may be in the colour or texture of the fabric or a combination of the elements which add up to style – perhaps the heel of the shoe, in height or width, is out of place, or the style of hat and its fit with the wig is oddly proportioned. With any luck it may only be in the simpler yet meaningful detail of accessories such as a handkerchief, handbag or gloves.

Creating period dress with a restricted budget can lead to problems in trying to unify the look when costumes are sourced through hire, borrowing and making. The designer needs to develop a disciplined eye. Controlling the colour palette, keeping reins on style, and harmonizing material and texture can be an agonizing business when sources are varied.

Period dress often restricts the actor's movement. However, some restriction on physical movement may tell more of the story.

Actors are expected to behave in a particular manner in accordance with period dress, but it is unlikely the audience will appreciate all period aesthetics. Therefore the designer needs to seek out the essentials – the elements that really matter.

The attitude of Lady Bracknell is exhibited in her severe dress with its black and silver-grey tones. Patricia Kneale in The Importance of Being Earnest.
Director: Michael Winter.
Lighting: Bernard Shaw. Mercury Theatre

More severe fashion trends meet those with less structure and more ease. The cast in **The Importance of Being Earnest.**
Director: Michael Winter. Lighting: Bernard Shaw. Mercury Theatre

Consider what elements of dress indicate an aristocrat, judge, tailor, artist, gardener or maid. Which accessories would help to communicate these positions and practices? How much of a historical or traditional image can be sacrificed and what manners and behaviours could be introduced to emphasize and support the characterization? Consider a basic contemporary style of dress to which you add period details. Balance out silhouette proportionally with slight exaggeration to heighten the effect. A little exaggeration gives the look a theatrical edge, and works within the convention of the theatre.

Design that places emphasis on silhouette and avoids elaborating on decorative period detail can have a powerful effect on the audience through its boldness and simplicity, and may prove less costly. With simplification, the quality of cut and fit needs be of a high standard as more attention will be paid to the fit. In minimizing decoration, the audience's attention is also more substantially directed towards the face and its expression, to gesture, and to manners.

The Craft of Illusion

Theatre is filled with illusion. Audiences can be tricked and fooled – they can be led to believe in things which are not totally real. Things on-stage, more often than not, are not what they seem. Special effects support the craft of illusion-making. These may be lighting and sound, or painted, applied and constructed effects. Making heavy canvas appear as leather requires treatments of paint, dye, wax and polish to successfully deceive the eye. Thick felt with a resin/fibreglass coating can appear as metal armour. Lighting is all important in creating illusion out of crafted costume.

Foundations

Constraints of the period are sometimes a help and at times a hindrance to the actor. Design takes a leap off the page with fitting the undergarments. The movements and manners that result from wearing constructed shapes becomes the main focus from then onwards. It is important that the actor is both at ease and comfortable in their costume. However, the high quality of tailoring and making these days usually ensures that this is the case.

Adding exaggerated weight through padding or with cage constructs needs to be balanced with the proportions and bony structure of the actor. The neck and face, wrists and hands are tell-tale signs of an actor's own shape. Complex latex prosthetics, which enlarge the area, can be applied to areas such as the chin and neck but the natural movements become restricted. Building up too layered a disguise in make-up and costume may jeopardize the performance.

Historical silhouettes are frequently quite exaggerated and the understructuring appropriate to the period should be understood thoroughly before making is considered.

Constructing Breathable Undergarments

The actor naturally finds stage lighting extremely hot. Breathability is very important and design must be sympathetic to this.

Achieving an increase of stomach mass can be quite challenging. There are the obvious choices of wadding or padding to fatten an actor. This proves successful when the actor is in

---

Note

Knowledge about period cut and construction frequently comes through taking on design projects and researching them. The process of learning becomes all the more engaging when you have real problems at hand. Applying yourself to the concerns of the play gives you reason to investigate period costume. Aspects of shape, tailoring and construction then become more real, through having a purpose to use them. Period detail becomes more interesting when applied to a character. This is a more appropriate approach to understanding period than just reading about it as an independent study in itself. It is much more of a challenge and a thrill to learn through doing.

---

costume for short periods of time. The alternative is making cage constructs out of flexible ribbing. This approach can prove both visually successful and cool for the actor. As with the crinoline, air can circulate freely within and around the body.

Costumes which appear as clothing. Comfortable and easy to wear. A group design where the look of each character needs to complement the others. Photo: Roger Howard. *The cast on-stage.* Albert Herring. *Guildhall School of Music and Drama*

Layered effects, although very interesting visually, can also become hot to wear. In this case, undergarments such as waistcoats, knitted pullovers and shirts can have their backs removed. Anything that becomes hidden with overgarments may be cut out – sleeves, for example, may be removed with the cuff remaining as a separate piece. In some cases they may be attached to the lining of the jacket, with the cuff end extending beyond the jacket sleeve. Cutting away the back of a waistcoat only requires tie-offs to cross the back to keep it in place.

EXAMPLES OF PERIOD DRESS

The Gothic Knight

During the twelfth century gothic fashion refined its moral position to women in Europe. The female was honoured by the knight, who pledged an honourable service of women. The rules, which are described in The Pictorial Encyclopaedia of Fashion (see Bibliography), state that during courtship a knight, in love, follows four colour-coded stages of dress in order to be united with his loved one.

First the knight errant wears green so to attain courage to confess his love.

Declaring his love to the lady, he then wears white, a symbol of hopeful longing.

On favourable hearing with his lady and with his services accepted, he then wears red.

With returned affection from his lady his happiness is expressed by wearing yellow.

An Excess of Style in Germany

This quote is from an Austrian chronicler in fourteenth- and fifteenth-century Germany

Everyone dressed as he pleased. Some had the left sleeve much wider than the right – wider even than the length of the whole coat – while others wore sleeves of equal width. Some again embroidered the left sleeve in various ways, with ribbons of all colours or with silver bugles threaded on silk strings. Some wore on the breast a kerchief of various colours embroidered with letters in silver and silk. Still others wore pictures on their left breast. Some had clothes made so long they could not dress or undress without assistance, or without undoing a multitude of small buttons dispersed all over the sleeve, the breast, and

Costume offering fullness to character without the exaggerations becoming too ridiculous.
Humphrey in Knight of the Burning Pestle.

The formal Mr Vik, who seems quite at home in his period dress. Drawing of actor Bernard Hopkins for Enemy of the People.
Director: Martha Henry

the abdomen. Some added to their clothes hems of cloth of a different colour; others replaced these hems by numerous points and scallops. Everyone wore hoods...

SHOES IN 1480

The shoe in 1480 reached a fashionable peak. The pointed toe of the shoe extended to excessive lengths – often three times the foot's length. A special under-shoe made of wood was required to reinforce the shape and maintain the fit. A wire structure held the point in its position.

A duke or prince wore the point at two and a half times the foot's length. Members of the aristocracy wore the point twice the foot's length.

Tip

The details of costume accessory are everything. The right cigarette case, the perfect fan, the pocket just the right size and in the right place, the way the collar sits. The costume lives and breathes in its detail. The cut and fabric are just the start: from there the great designer puts the personality of the costume and hence the character into its detail. I don't mean fussiness.

Martha Henry

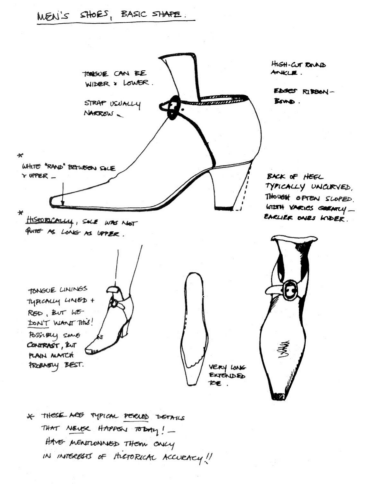

Historically informative sketches for men's shoes in Love for Love.
Designer Ann Curtis

Knights wore the point at one and a half times the foot's length. The rich wore the extended point a foot length beyond. Common people wore the point half a foot length beyond the toe. On stage, even without the wood addition, this fashion would prove quite challenging, highly amusing yet distracting. As a stylized gesture for a minor comic character, it might have possibility. It could fit into a bold expressionist design although it may be difficult to find the play to merit it.

Playwrights frequently elaborate on fashion and manners of dress. In Shakespeare's *Twelfth Night*, Malvolio appears in a guise to romantically impress Olivia. He is misguided into believing the fashionable trend of cross-gartering is acceptable within the upper classes. His elaborate display of below the knee cross-gartering becomes a complete affront to Olivia, much to his deep disappointment and embarrassment. Poor Malvolio is made to look quite humiliated.

9 WIGS, HAIRSTYLES AND MAKE-UP

Hairstyles play a significant role in complementing costume and defining character. Character and period are clearly linked with style of hair. Hairstyles can be quite clearly dated. Designs which incorporate contemporary aesthetics into period hairstyle cause concern, for they display inaccurate interpretations, and are therefore misleading – note films of a classic genre made between the 1940s and 1960s. Audiences are becoming increasingly familiar with and informed by history, its modes and manners. We all have access to and are familiar with photography since the 1840s, as well as historical painted portraits, fashion plates and illustrations, and professionally produced period films.

To the audience, the actor's head and face are the main focus throughout a performance. Like costume, hair is viewed from all angles. It is crucial that the actor's facial features be seen. When actors speak through hair, when the hair obscures the face, the result is talking hair. Most problems arise when the actor is in profile. Without being able to see clearly the expressive features of the face, the audience lose interest in what a character is saying.

Costume drawings need to suggest period shape and style in hair and wigs. Historically, proportions in hair tend to complement the proportions found in costume. Period hair is often a construct, it has understructure, it is made of dressed pieces, and it has incorporated into it

decoration and millinery that are fashioned together to create the look. Some looks are extremely complex constructs. Actors are keenly concerned over how they will wear their hair. The colour, the way it is dressed and the accessories to

Fashion plate from The Queen,
The Ladies Newspaper, 1880.

87

go with it are all important. When wigs are called for it is essential that the fit be appropriate to the head wearing it. An ill-fitting wig will make the actor feel insecure and affect their performance.

Make-up brings the hair or wig and face together. When a character's hair colour differs from the actor's own, make-up is applied to bridge the imbalance. Make-up can successfully change one face into another.

Explanations or illustrations of hairstyle may require the designer to produce additional drawings to accompany the costume drawings. Such drawings offer front, side and rear views of hair. It may also prove helpful for the wig department if additional period research is included.

WIGS AND HAIRSTYLES

With historical dress, it is recommended to follow through with accuracy in hairstyle. Designs that are eclectic, those which pool together different periods, allow more room for creativity. Historical hairstyles need to work for the actor. The wig must complement the head and face wearing it. Some imagination needs to be applied to interpreting period accuracy, so the style looks appropriate for the individual.

Decisions over whether to dress the actor's own hair, hire or make a wig, is guided often by finance. Commercially available wigs, seemingly appropriate for dressing, are not so easy to convert into period styles. Wigs made for the theatre are expensive, but look realistic. Hire costs are generally on a weekly basis.

The actor needs to attend several fittings at the wig makers. This calls for scheduling and careful planning. Some actors' contracts allow for a limited number of costume and wig fittings. Over and above these numbers may mean paying them extra. Of course, fitting out the whole cast in wigs would be very expensive, usually beyond the budget of most

Fashion plate from **The Queen,** *The Lady's Newspaper, 1880.*

Wig and hat details for Tattle in Love For Love.
Designer: Ann Curtis.
Stratford Festival Theatre

designers. It is at times like this that ingenuity must come to the fore. A hat or bonnet, turban or cap may prove the ideal, cost-effective way around using a wig. Sometimes small additions of featured hair are attached to the head gear. However, the disadvantage of this is that any slight shift of the hat on the head also shifts the hair, which would be character destroying.

Look carefully at the cast members as early as possible, even if it is only their photographs. If possible, make a special trip to meet the actors and take along a camera. Once they are contracted, advise them not to have any haircuts, unless they have spoken to you first. It is an unfortunate situation

when, on the first day of rehearsal, they show up with an unexpected short crop of hair.

When using wigs, take into account the theatre space and audience distance. The close proximity of a thrust stage or theatre-in-the-round offers one challenge, while the proscenium and its divide creates another. Aim to control what the audience will focus on. Plan to emphasize the essential.

Whilst most actors prefer to use their own hair, styled for the part, they will usually be happy to use a good wig when the designs show a well-developed character. Wigs tend to be hot beneath the glare of theatre lights.

Dressing the actor's own hair appropriately for wearing a wig involves a planned procedure. Lengths of hair are coiled, pressed flat against the head, then pinned flat. The hair needs to be clean yet not freshly washed – the hair should be washed in the morning rather than in the evening prior to the show. Once pinned flat, a fine

Wig, cap, spectacles, coat and shirt collar.
Edward Atienza as Foresight. Love For Love.
Designer: Ann Curtis. Stratford Festival Theatre

Eccentric wigs and outrageuous costumes for Mr and Mrs Twit in **The Twits.** *Actors Kate Arneil and Chris Lavner.*
Director: Paul Harman.
Lighting: Martin Seymour. Unicorn Theatre

stocking is stretched over the hair and head. This is then pinned into place along its outer edges where it meets the hairline. This firm foundation supports any wig being pinned on to it.

Commercially made wigs can be of either real or synthetic hair, and there are a good choice of styles, cuts, lengths and colours. They are on an elastic base, which when worn gives good air circulation through to the scalp. Wigs made of synthetic hair may prove impossible to reshape, curl, wave, colour or alter in cut. Those with natural hair will offer more options for dressing. The disadvantage of elastic-base wigs lies in the style and appearance at the forehead hairline. It is unlikely you will be able to re-style the manufactured fall of hair along this line. These wigs show their worst

Wigs for Alan Scarf (left) and Barbara Bryne (centre) while Ted Dykstra (left) has his own hair shaped for the part in **Entertaining Mr Sloane.** *Director: David William. Lighting: John Munro. Stratford Festival Theatre. Courtesy of the Stratford Festival Theatre*

characteristics when the front hairline edge is in view. If your actor happens to have long hair which matches the wig colour it may be possible to incorporate their own hairline into the front of the wig.

Wig Hire

Before hiring a wig, you will need to make the following measurements:

1. Measure from the centre front hairline up over the top of the head to the back nape (base hairline at the neck).
2. Measure from the top of the ear across the top of the head to the top of the other ear.
3. Measure from the line of the side temple hairline around the back of the head to the other side temple hairline.
4. Measure from the front of the ear across the forehead to the centre front hairline across to the front of the other ear.
5. Measure around the head with the measure sitting above the ear taking in the circumference with the measure touching on the centre front hairline and the nape hairline.

Wig Maintenance

Wig maintenance throughout the run of a show requires careful planning. It is not always possible for the actor to attend to this, nor is it their responsibility, although in some instances, such as in small-scale and some medium-scale touring shows, the actors do attend to these matters. Heat affects the wig's dressing and by the end of a long show wigs can look quite relaxed and dishevelled. Wigs clog up with hair spray, they begin to shine, and soon turn into a lacquered mass. A wig dresser should regularly wash, re-style and dress the wig. Wigs of real hair usually need this doing for every show. When hiring a wig, take maintenance notes from the wig maker. Never wash, dress or re-style a hired wig without prior consent. When not in use, the wig needs to be placed on a wig block. Tailor-made wigs require blocks of the exact head size of the actor.

Professional Wig Making

Wig making is a skilled craft. At the first visit a measured skull cap is made. This cap is then fitted on to a block of corresponding size, and measurements are detailed out on the cap. Hair choice is from either human or animal sources. Colour, texture and the strand lengths are decided upon. Strand lengths will often differ in one wig from 15–50cm (6–20in). When observing natural hair colour, one notices the range of colour in one head of hair. This variety also applies to wig making. Colours and shades are blended so to create a naturalistic look, with strands being dyed on site as required.

Over the block, gauze pieces are sewn together, to form the mesh base. Using a type of crochet hook, several hairs are knotted together into the gauze foundation, starting along the base lines of the wig and working up to the top. Along the centre front, a lace base is attached. This fine mesh fits snugly across the forehead, above and below the hairline. Knotting the hair here requires special skill and handling. The natural hairline is not a harsh line and it is important that the hair should give the impression of growing out of the head, so only one hair at a time is knotted into place in this area. The hair needs to be knotted in a specific direction, this gives indication of patterns of growth.

It may take between two and four days to knot a wig, longer for more complex, period wigs. Once complete, the wig is fitted on to the actor and cut or trimmed. It may then be set with rollers, heat crimped if necessary and dried. The next step is styling, often with the actor in the wig.

When dressing and fitting wigs, notify the millinery and props departments if hats, tiaras and crowns are also to be worn. Collaboration is everything in making the actor's face, wig and millinery harmonize.

Hair Spray

Avoid using hair spray or lacquer when the wig is on the actor. Instead set the wig on the block in a well-ventilated room, then spray. Allow it to dry and then fit the wig. This is especially important when fitting wigs on opera singers. The sprays are particularly hazardous to the throat and voice.

Dressing

If a wig is being worn, costumes should be removed by ways other than over the head. Discuss alternative constructions and fastenings with wardrobe. For quick costume changes, be careful not to affect the look of the dressed hair and make-up. The actor who reappears from a costume change with dishevelled hair suggests another story. Quick changes requiring a dresser need be well planned and rehearsed with the wardrobe and wig department.

Changing Hair Colour

Actors may show interest in dying and professionally styling their own hair. Colour sprays are not recommended for changing the total hair colour. Sprays are best used sparingly, as highlight and shading. When considering dying the actors' hair, you need to consider how suitable their hair type is for a colour change and for their hair to take on the characteristics of the intended period style. Dark hair must be bleached to lighten it: few actors are willing to have their hair bleached.

Professional hair products are readily available which tint and colour fair hair, which can then be dyed dark quite easily. It is recommended that a professional stylist take charge of such matters. Discuss restoration methods, and schedule in appointments at the end of the run to restore the actors' hair to its original colour. Remember to take any associated costs into account.

Hair and Wig Whiteners

Liquid creme, powder and spray are used to grey out and whiten the hair. Brush or comb into the hair, building up the effect slowly. Take care to make the effect as realistic as possible. An artificial look is all too easily achieved when the roots are neglected. Work it well down into the hair and be sure not to overdo it when ageing a young actor. Shampooing the hair will remove powders.

FACIAL HAIR

Facial hair consists of beards, sideboards (sideburns), moustaches, eyebrows and eyelashes. Facial hair is knotted on to a fine lace mesh which is attached to the face with spirit gum or adhesive. The gum is applied to the skin, aired to become tacky, then the lace is applied. The mesh may be lifted from the face by using spirit gum remover.

MR. DAVID FOX

DR. STOCKMAN

MR. NICHOLAS PENNEL

MAJOR

DRY - TIMID - STAUNCH CONSERVATIVE

3 PIECE MATCHING LOUNGE SUIT
TWEED BROWN

DR. STOCKTIAN

KATHRINE

WARM - AFFECTIONATE

COMFORTABLE - AT EASE -
WITHOUT PRETENTION.

Preliminary sketches for finding the face for a character, with suggestions for hairstyle, facial hair, and costume.
Enemy of the People

Actors can create their own facial hair by applying crepe hair. This may be used to make moustaches, eyebrows, sideboards and even beards. Crepe hair is cheap and available in braided strands. The actor should try to match the colour with his own hair, remembering the colour of facial hair is often slightly different from head hair. Crepe hair may be straightened by steaming it with an iron or stretching it out whilst wet and blow drying.

Spirit gum is applied to the face, aired to become tacky, then the crepe is applied in small amounts at a time. Apply the gum only in the area you are immediately working on. Consider the growth direction of hair. The alternative to spirit gum is a professional latex-based glue specifically designed for the face,

A cap on the head and a shawl over the hair help to pull focus to the face. These accessories complement the costume, and add support to these charming rural characters.
Stephan Loges and Katija Dragojevic on-stage in Albert Herring.
Director: Thomas de Mallet Burgess. Lighting: Kevin Sleep. Guildhall School of Music and Drama. Photo: Roger Howard

but this is better used in larger areas like the beard. Trim the crepe hair to the required length after the adhesive has fully set.

Any application of glue should be on to a clean, greaseless skin. The face should be washed thoroughly with soap or cleansed with a degreasing agent. All make-up should be applied after facial hair is attached and should be completed before the wig is placed on the head. When wearing a lace front wig, avoid applying make-up to the forehead until the wig is in place. Then touch up with make-up around

the hairline, over the lace, where the lace edge meets the forehead.

Fix down wigs and facial hair securely. Rushed preparation puts the actor into a sweat, which offers a poor foundation for secure adhesion. Excessive facial movement may cause facial hair to separate from the face. Intervals may enable the actor to adjust and re-fix wigs and facial hair.

MAKE-UP

Functions of Make-Up
1. To enable features to project themselves out and across the space within which the audience sits. The size of the auditorium dictates how much make-up should be used.
2. To make corrections, balance, harmonize or beautify the actor's own features.
3. To alter an actor's features to achieve a particular effect.

Realistic Make-Up
Realistic make-up is that which fits the artificial conventions of staged drama. Although its aim may be to appear natural, there is generally a measure of artifice involved. Characters may appear naturalistic, yet they may have undergone some transformation to achieve this. Non-made-up faces read as expressive if the theatre is intimate. Under intense theatre lighting and coloured gels, the face without make-up may well offer a well-sculpted, balanced and coloured impression.

Distances between the stage and audience reduce ease of recognition. The challenge is to achieve a realistic image which projects itself through to the back seats yet does not become artificial for those in the near front. Characters are unique through their differences – their age, weight, features, skin type, colouring, hair characteristics and style. Realism attempts to depict the very spirit of character.

Symbolic Make-up

Symbolizm in make-up accepts the realism of character yet presents it as a collective symbol. This tends to emphasize basic character traits through the forms of abstraction which symbolize them. A mask is a more obvious form of a symbolic image. Masks seek to abstract the realities, to simplify or intensify particular aspects of the inner self. Simplicity has great power in symbolism. The demands made on the imagination in the viewer are increased. Free from an actor's features and the intimate scale of a face, symbolizm re-constructs to put a more direct image into play.

Approaching Make-Up

Dress rehearsals offer time to critically analyse make-up, wigs, hairstyles and costumes. Every opportunity on-stage under lights proves valuable. Consider sitting in different positions in the auditorium to better observe the results. The surrounding elements of set and lighting design have a considerable effect on the appearance of the actor. It can also be very helpful to observe the visual impact of the actors as a group. Alterations in the lighting levels will affect the look of make-up. A heavy make-up which ages a character may look acceptable under low light levels, however when the intensity is increased it may well appear too artificial. It is often thought that if you notice the actor is wearing make-up, then the make-up is too obvious.

Highlight and Shadow

Stage lighting hits the face of the actor from various directions. The illumination will naturally flatten out the features – the face lit from just one source will create a more dynamic impression. Stage lighting directions are generally from above and to the sides. Footlights are sometimes introduced, but usually only as specials.

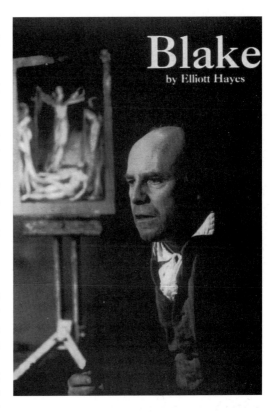

Michael Loughnan playing William Blake. Michael's own look needed little adjustment, but some beard stubble, dishevelled hair at the sides and back, along with a well-worn costume added to the success of the look. A pale base make-up added enough age, and a dirty make-up rubbed into the hands and fingernails added character. William Blake. Director: Valerie Doulton. Tristan Bates Theatre. Photo: Simon Annand

Painting into the face produces highlight and shadow, adds colour change, texture and line. Proportions can be altered and emphasized. Bony structure can be defined and or reshaped through applications of highlight and shadow. The nose and chin can undergo a painterly change to lengthen, shorten, vary width, sharpen or soften.

Ageing an actor usually demands less make-up than one thinks. When it looks artificial it is not believable. Take into account the natural bony structure of the face you wish to age. In a younger face, the flesh may be handsomely disguising the inner bony shape. When this face ages, the bony structure becomes more pronounced. Feel around the face for those bones which are to be emphasized. It may be more believable to age the face along its own natural contours. Have references from your research at hand. Avoid painting in lines and concentrate more on surface shaping in terms of light and dark areas. Keep the lines to a minimum and not in a heavy hand. The points to stress are light and shade in facial features, and in the loss of colour that comes with ageing.

Shading and shadows should be applied initially with the foundation or base. All lighter shading in colour and with highlight should be added afterwards. Highlights will appear muddy if put directly over the painted shadow. Apply them alongside the shadow area, blending with a make-up brush. Once the main areas are base coloured and blended together, then begin work on areas around the eyes and mouth using make-up pencils, mascara and eye shadow.

When applying lines to age the face, seriously consider the distance of the audience. Painted shadows and highlights should do most of the work to age a face. Like an egg in shadow, the highlight is above the shading which moves into the shadow with the line as a final deep recess to imply the fold of skin. Lightly applied lines, blended into the shadow area will make them more convincing. Look at aged wrinkled faces for reference.

Exercise
Set up an anglepoise lamp and a mirror. Have a good look at your face under the direction of one light source. Cast the lighting down from different angles. Take photographs of the

> ## Tip
>
> I talk to the designer about make-up especially if the design is very flamboyant or of a period that calls for something special. Finally, I prefer to develop my own make-up as it's the element that transforms my face into the face that becomes 'her'. The thing I dislike most about film (and I love making films) is that someone else does my face. I say to myself 'This is a part of this process – this is the way this goes'. I don't understand having someone else do your make-up on-stage, I'm not used to it, it's part of my ritual. Make-up has become less blatant over the years, affected by lighting and attitudes. It is hard to find an actor who uses either pan-cake or sticks. I now almost never use false eyelashes or even mascara, whereas it used to be a pretty standard thing.
>
> **Martha Henry**

results to show how your features look as pronounced. Note the sculptural quality of your own face. Note the shadows cast to the side and underside of features. Make the light harsh or brilliant, then try to soften the glare by moving away from the light source. Note the colour of the shadow tones especially as they relate to the skin colour nearer the light.

Take an object such as an egg and do the same. Note the fall of the shadow on the egg. Note the levels of intensity and depth of shadow. Note that the interplay of light creates the sculptural form. Lighting an egg from above and from both sides will flatten out its sculptural form making you believe it could be a cut-out flat egg shape. The shadow colouring will be relative to the object colour.

Exercise
Use soft charcoal and compressed charcoal to draw some faces. Draw on pastel or heavy

cartridge paper which has a tooth to its surface. Aim to develop an understanding for sculptural form. Concentrate on light and shade. Avoid line drawing. Make the flesh tone a light grey, or choose a grey paper – this eliminates the brilliant white page and in fact cuts a corner. Think of light and dark charcoal as the modelling medium. Sculpt the form through highlights, shading and shadow. Add a compressed white chalk to your kit for adding in highlights. When working on white paper, an eraser is a tool for creating highlight, it restores the white of the page. Art shops offer a tool for rubbing and blending made of compressed soft paper. It comes like a very fat pencil and is ideal for smoothing out the charcoal and graduating shades.

Skin Colouring

Flesh tones differ within each race. Flesh colouring leans towards specific areas on the colour wheel. We see pink and red faces, those with warm brown or yellow tinges, the cooler complexions, the bronzed and golden. The paler skin tones look rather ghost-like on stage and require an opaque base and colour to reflect the light. The less coloured flesh tones may wash out and therefore need a warmer tone colour applied. Beneath coloured lighting gels actors' complexions will again either cool down or heat up, depending on the colour of gel. The kind and amount of stage light makes a great difference to make-up. Each production has its own unique problems. Richly coloured skin requires careful highlighting in make-up that blends with the natural colouring.

A dark base make-up applied to the face could well be considered the shadow and everything applied to this would thereafter be highlight. Light reflects highlight not shadow. To build up from shadow emphasizing what the audience tends to see is a reasonable way to approach it. Additional shadows applied afterwardstend to be limited to fine lines. It is

Wig and actor's own facial hair, with drag make-up and a revealed chest of hair.

easier to shade down too much highlight than it is to lighten the areas of shadow.

Basic Make-Up

Pan-Cake
This greaseless foundation, which comes in a range of colours, requires application with a damp make-up sponge. Using even strokes, apply a thin coating over the face, ears, and parts of the neck which are exposed. Use the

97

White base make-up with heavily accented eyes and lips help make this curious character all the more of a collage oddity. Collage for The Rocky Horror Show

clean side of the sponge to blend the colour evenly while the face is still wet. Pan-Cake dries to an even, matt surface. You need not apply powder because of the natural dryness of the foundation. However, actors who perspire excessively may wish to lightly powder to compensate.

Creme make-up

This is found in a range of colours, and may be applied using a brush, sponge or with the fingertips. Keep to a thin layer over the skin surface. Creme make-up is non-greasy but has the same sheen as pan-stick greasepaint. The natural satin finish requires a powder dusting to be sponged over afterwards to produce a dry finish. Remove excess powder with a brush.

Pan-Stick

A greasepaint in hard stick form. Colours should be rubbed into the palm of the hand and blended before being applied. Once the satisfactory colour is achieved, rub both palms together and then smooth in the colour to the areas of the face as required. The satin finish of greasepaint requires a powder overlay, which takes the shine off the skin surface. Pat it on over the face until the base appears dry. Excess powder may be brushed away with a powder brush. Pan-stick requires a cold creme make-up foundation on the face to ensure colour blending.

Greasepaint

Available in tubes, jars or sticks, greasepaint gives coloured skin tone. Colours are easily mixed together either in the palm of the hand or by applying dots of colour to the areas required and blending them together on the face. A base foundation on dry skin makes the application and blending easier. Greasepaint has good covering power, hiding natural skin defects and blemishes. If the skin is unusually dry, a thin cold cream base should be applied

underneath. Greasepaint requires a powder overlay afterwards due to its sheen.

Make-up pencil

A greasepaint pencil available in a range of colours. Ideal for creating definition to eyebrows and adding in lines. To sharpen the pencil tip use a sharp cutting blade.

Mascara

Used to add definition to the eyelashes as well the fine hairs along the hairline when required.

Eye shadow

Coloured make-up cakes, sticks and greasepaints will do for this, so avoiding the costly alternatives.

Face powder

Once all the shading, blending and softening of lines has been done and rouge applied, the face is powdered. Powdering the face all over with a velvet pad removes sheen, its transparent nature does not alter the make-up colouring.

Start with the neck and chin area and work progressively up, patting the face with a firm hand. Cover over all the paint make-up. Once complete, finish off by brushing the face over with a powder brush. Any shiny areas will require more powder.

Make-Up Removal

Recommended removers for particular products are worth investigating prior to purchase of any make-up. The greasepaint make-ups are removed with cleansing creams such as cold cream.

Hypo-allergenic products are available as well as those without perfumes or scents. Oils are preferred by some actors, baby oil being one such product – ideal for sensitive skins. The non-greasy make-ups such as pan-cake are easily washed off with soap and warm water.

CONSTRUCTIONS FOR THE FACE

Latex Constructs

This technique is both involved and very time consuming, yet it produces remarkable results. It can produce major transformations of an actor's face and head shape. Complete transformations can be achieved to make an actor look like another person. The constructs are lightweight latex foam pieces that adhere to the actor's face, fitting comfortably, like a glove. From the outside, the features of the actor will be transformed. This effect is generally made up of many individual parts: it is not a solid mask. The parts adhere separately so the facial muscles remain flexible.

The technique and skill is a professional business and should not be attempted by the student without some background reading on the subject and seeing it being done. In making any form of moulded impression of a face, it is essential that the appropriate steps are taken to ensure the person is able to breathe properly at all times during the procedure. This is especially true when the process goes partially wrong, as the situation could become life-threatening.

First, a mould of the actor's face and head are made using an appropriate casting plaster. In some instances this is applied in parts, with the top of the head being cast as a separate piece. The face front and neck will be another part. They are fashioned to fit together once the mould is set. Once removed from the head of the actor these solid pieces are the moulds, the inside of which is the 'negative' impression of the actor's head and face. Plaster is then poured into the shell, left to dry and then the inner casting is removed. The cast is a solid life mask of the actor.

The life mask is then built upon, sculpting it into the features of the desired character. When complete, a mould is made by again by applying casting plaster to the head and face shape using the same method as before. The resulting mould is the 'negative' impression of the intended character.

Through a clever system of planned registrations the actor's life mask when placed inside the character mould fits and aligns itself into its correct position. The actual void between these two, or the space where they do not meet, are the areas that will be filled with foam latex. To achieve this, the two pieces are separated. The character mould, laid on a flat table surface, looks like a basin. Into this, foam latex is poured, and the actor's life mask is immediately pressed into its registration position. Excess foam flows out as waste. The whole thing is dried and the result when separated is the many facial parts to be individually applied to the actor's face.

Putty or Wax

A kneadable, sticky, pliable product ideal for building up areas such as the nose, eyebrow region and chin. This putty (or wax) is not ideal for too significant a build up due to its inflexible nature. It does not react well to too much facial expression and movement. Apply to grease-free skin after kneading it thoroughly with the fingers. Use a little petroleum jelly to make it more pliable and prevent it from adhering to the finger tips. To increase its staying power, apply a thin coat of spirit gum to the face and allow to air dry. Apply the putty, gently shape and mould it to the face. Any fine cracks can be filled with a small amount of petroleum jelly. A clear sealer may be required to 'join' the edge of the putty to the skin. The putty should be well shaped so the sealing agent acts to prevent it from cracking away from the skin. Make-up can then be applied to the putty: take care to do this gently so as not to affect the shape. If applying sealer or gum, be sure to use the recommended removers prior to removing the construct.

*A family photograph circa 1959, offering
valuable first-hand information about dress
and accessories, hair and make-up.*

Warts

These can be built up in the same way by using
the putty or wax as above. The spirit gum and
sealer may prove an advantage on oily skin types.

Ears

Ears may be built up and reshaped with putty
or wax if time is taken to mould it around the
surrounding natural ear shape. Ears may be
pushed forward with a build up of putty
behind the ear, but be sure that the actor's hair
masks or hides it. Blend in the putty to the
shape of the ear and surrounding head.

Scars

A liquid face latex may be painted on to the
skin and then manipulated while it dries to
form cuts and scars. Once dry, apply the base
foundation and colour to blend it into the skin,
adding blood colour and scab tissue colour
where necessary.

Another approach is to build up the effect
out of plastercine or wax directly on the face.
This is then removed and a mould is made by
covering over its face surface with fine dental
plaster or a dense casing rubber. You then
paint into the mould with a liquid latex,
building up a thickness with layers. Remove
the latex, flip it over and you have what you
started with initially. Be sure to use petroleum
jelly as a resist in the mould, a thin brushing
over the inside of the mould will ensure the
cast latex scar can be removed with ease. The
sculpted scar can be made again and again
from the same mould, which is particularly
useful when the show has a long run.

YOUR LIBRARY

Build up a scrapbook with photographs from
newspapers and magazines on the subject of
faces. Categorize and label sections such as old
age, middle age, youth, colour, race, and
beauty; expressions such as comic and tragic;
the eccentric and the humble face. Pay
particular attention to individual characteristics such as eyebrows, eyes, hairlines, ageing
and lines.

Look around you at family and older friends.
Check out their ages. Keep a collection of
photographs with age and dates noted. You
may be quite surprised to find that it is more a
change of texture that defines an older face
rather than an excess of lines. Age shows up
differently in the faces of different race types.
Premature ageing may be the result of some
influence such as an excess of worry, too much
alcohol, an illness or excessive exposure to
direct sunshine.

Many a play has characters that fall into
such categories. Look for what builds up
character in a face. Especially look for people
that work hard at manual labour either
indoors or outdoors. Look at other countries
and cultures for differences in the labour force.
Look at the leisurely too, and observe the
differences. Collect some history, however
brief, on the people themselves. Observe people
beneath overhead lighting, those cross-lit
indoors and outside, day and night.

10 FOUNDATIONS AND CHARACTERISTICS OF DESIGN

Almost everything that surrounds us – objects, clothing, even the meals we eat, is a product of design. Design is the creative end of the manufacturing process. Ideas which concern the appearance, as well as ideas as to how something should be made, come from designers.

Design evolves through the application of new ideas, materials and methods of manufacture. Ideas centred on an object's function may remain the same yet the form and its style may change. The concept of a vacuum cleaner may remain the same, but how it functions and how it looks will evolve.

Cultural differences affect how an object will look. The appearance of an object, one which serves a purpose, may differ significantly from one country to another according to conditions of manufacture and cultural aesthetics.

Design is a form of enquiry – it is an attitude. It is not a method to be learned and then practised. Design is a plan for order. It concerns itself with form in the most fundamental sense. It is about the markings made by tools, through medium and technique. Design is not an end in itself but more a way of making one more aware. To be effective, design needs to fulfil its purpose. When design is interesting it then shows individuality. However, the results of design are not in themselves an art form.

Design is full of reference to people, place and time. Design easily becomes dated or redundant yet it may successfully evolve into new forms. The challenges that shape design are often a condition of changing times and practical design needs to adapt to these demands.

Design serves a practical function, it has purpose. Therefore it is no surprise that designers are looking towards creating intelligent fabrics, with the aim of producing a fabric which has capacity to regulate itself, through being actively engaged with the body's changing temperature.

LINE

Line is a by-product, achieved through applying a tool or instrument to a material. The most common form is in pencil or ink on paper. Line is a series of dots that indicate direction. When in a sequence, they traverse the surface either by marking the top tooth surface or by etching themselves into the surface. Mark making may be temporary or permanent. Line creates boundaries and causes separation. All line has character. Line is used both by the plastic arts in sculpture and the graphic arts for surface work.

Line obtains style through its references. It may be lyrical and rhythmic. Line adapts itself to suit its function. The lines of a car are both aerodynamic and aesthetic. For the artist and designer, line becomes their signature. The quality of line used by Van Gogh is unlike that of any other artist. Design exhibits a sense of stylish line. The technique employed to create line, along with how the medium is handled, produces a style.

TEXTURE

The outer surface of an object has unique and particular characteristics. This is the surface character of substance. The way in which light falls across a surface tells us something about it. We become more familiar with objects through recognizing the texture by touch. The sensory experience is extremely valuable when learning. We are continually discovering something new about texture, forming strong opinions about our likes and dislikes.

Line and texture are inseparable. Texture is automatically created when a line is drawn. It becomes the by-product of the process of mark-making and is therefore unavoidable. Texture is characteristically smooth or rough. Texture in drawing is characterized by the volume surface-state and from the medium and materials employed.

Texture can be clearly suggested with economy while drawing. A little of it goes a long way when describing something. Texture does not need to cover all the surface planes in a drawing to inform us of its nature and existence. The drawn line alone can express texture. Think of a woolly line, a feathery line, a rugged line, a silky line – the stroke of a line is evidence of texture.

Texture is a sensation we perceive and respond to with immediacy. How a surface appears can tell us either to approach or to take a step back. Knowledge of texture is something we learn through experience. You only need to touch a sea urchin or poison ivy once to know to avoid it thereafter. Once the skin has felt cashmere, rougher wool becomes less desirable. Texture has strong characteristics associated with people, place and time. People and race can be described through textural references.

Texture creates spatial relationships. It defines, separates and proposes volume. It can create the illusion of three dimensions. Texture adds interest to area and can be used to describe the effect of light upon a surface to stimulate tactile responses. A blurring of textural detail may suggest distance. Texture focused and sharply defined may appear to advance towards the eye.

An over-emphasis of textural interest within one area can detract from the harmony and overall appreciation of the whole. Excessive texture may become no more than visual padding. Pattern may then appear as purely decorative. Texture may enhance the emotional experience. It adds feeling to form and heightens the associative relationships of memory, time and place. It is advisable to use texture in careful harmony with other design elements. When used functionally it speaks volumes.

Frottage

Place a thin sheet of paper over any surface and rub with a pencil or chalk. This textural transfer is called frottage. Brass rubbings are a form of frottage. It is useful to collect a scrapbook of textured rubbings, each individually labelled. Try frottage on hard and soft textured surfaces.

COLOUR

Colour is like texture in that it stimulates the senses. We react or respond to colour emotionally. Our relationship with colour becomes personal through experience. Our culture, geography and relationships with neighbouring countries teaches us a lot about what we know of colour.

Experiments in colour need to be a first-hand experience. Have fun experimenting with colour and trust your senses when forming an opinion – initial judgements of colour should be subjective. Let your instinctive reactions measure up against those reactions to colour which are taught. Feelings can also affect our judgement of colour.

Colour theory supports all aspects of design and can be easily learned. Artists appreciate colour both intuitively and intellectually; developing and nurturing unique relationships with colour, its mixing and blending, its inter-relationships. The purpose in exercises with colour is to become familiar with its properties, characteristics and capacity. Becoming familiar with the colour wheel is the basic starting point.

The Uses of Colour

1. To give spatial quality to a pictorial field.
2. To create mood and symbolize idea.
3. To provide a vehicle for the expression of personal emotions and feelings.
4. To attract attention as a means of giving organization to composition.
5. To attain aesthetic appeal through a system of ordered colour relationships.
6. To identify by describing the superficial fact of appearance.

Dimensional Effects Through Using Colour

1. Contrast of brightness against darkness.
2. Contrast of using pure hue against grey colours.
3. Contrast of warm colours against cool colours.
4. Contrast of detail and texture against planes of flat areas.
5. To imply continuation of design background seen running behind foreground elements.
6. Highlights and shadows.

Objective colour

That which is intrinsic or local. The natural colour of an object as it is seen by the eye.

Subjective colour

The expressive use of colour, without regard to natural appearance. That which is ambiguous or decorative, chosen as invention by designers and artists.

Primary colours

The purest forms of colour, which cannot be broken down into any other hues. The fundamental triad of red, yellow and blue form an equilateral triangle on the colour wheel.

THE COLOUR WHEEL

The colour wheel consists of twelve colours – yellow, yellow-orange, orange, orange-red, red, red-violet, violet, violet-blue, blue, blue-green, green, and green-yellow.

It is advisable to draw the wheel, as illustrated, into your sketchbook using a compass. Follow through by painting the colours on to a separate sheet of watercolour paper. When dry, these can be cut out and pasted on to the wheel. This allows for experimentation off the finished sketchbook page, which allows some room for trial and error.

Lay out the primary colours – red, yellow, blue. Green may be made by mixing yellow and blue or purchased as a spectrum hue.

Add in the colours orange and violet, produced by mixing yellow and red, and blue and red respectively. Make mixtures for the intermediate colours – red-orange, yellow-orange, yellow-green, blue-green, blue-violet, and red-violet. The twelve hues are now established.

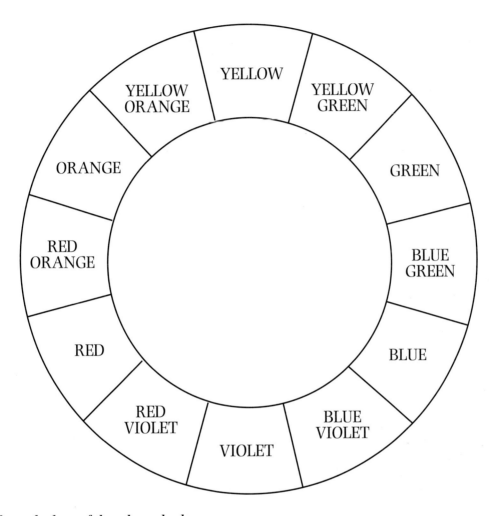

The twelve hues of the colour wheel.

HUE, VALUE AND INTENSITY

These three qualities must be taken into account when describing any colour.

The hue is the chromatic quality of a colour as indicated by its name. To change the hue of a colour, we need to mix another colour with it. Yellow mixed with orange becomes yellow-orange, this is a change in hue. On the colour wheel, twelve hues are represented. Limiting the numbers makes the differences distinguishable. Hue is the pure spectrum colour at its most brilliant.

The relation of colour to white and black is indicated by value, and is expressed in terms of 'light' or 'dark'. This places the colour in high or low value to its normal spectrum colour. To alter the value we mix in something lighter or darker. We do not change the hue of colour by mixing in white or black, only its value is altered.

Create a chart with black and white placed at the extremes. Place the mixings of seven

105

values between. The centre value becomes mid-grey. Between black and mid-grey you have intermediate dark. To either side of this, you will have low dark and high dark. Between white and mid-grey you have intermediate light, and on either side you will have low light and high light.

The full intensity of a hue is found at its strongest note, saturation or chroma. We differentiate by saying a brilliant red or a dull red. To change the intensity of a hue, we mix in the neutral grey found at the centre of the colour wheel. Neutral grey is achieved through the mixing of any two comp-lementary colours. (*See* complementary colours, page 107.)

Make a value chart with neutral grey and a hue at the extremes. Place between them degrees of change indicating variable intensities of that hue.

The fullness of intensity for any hue can occur at only one value. Yellow when made darker by neutral grey still retains its fullest intensity for yellow at that value. Take two yellows, one at full saturation, and the other at the same value but half the intensity. Pass shadows over these two, this creates a darkened effect relative to intermediate dark on the scale of values. The yellow will be less intense for both, yet the one which was most intense in the previous light will be at its fullest intensity in shadow, with the other remaining half intense as before.

TRANSMITTED AND REFLECTED LIGHT

Transmitted light through a leaf shows brilliant colour. Colour may also be a made brilliant through light that is reflected off the surface. However colour is more intense when light is transmitted through the translucent material or matter.

Almost all materials and substances absorb light. Absorption of light into the surface texture affects the colour that we see. The colour we see comes through both surface absorption and reflected light. White light projected through a prism reveals the spectrum colours that unite to form white light. Substances absorb different combin-ations of these coloured rays. Those that are absorbed are the rays that coloured substance lacks in prism colour. The rays that are sent back to the eye are those that the substance has in degrees as part of its nature. These rays are the reflected or unabsorbed spectrum colours.

Substances only reflect or transmit colours found in the light rays that are projected upon them. A red fabric will absorb all white light rays except the red rays, reflecting them back to the eye. With a light projection containing no red rays, such as blue-green, the cloth will appear grey or black: its surface will also reflect back some of the blue-green as colour. This difference of absorption and reflection of coloured rays enables designers to paint a scene that under light of a certain hue appears in one compositional way, but when the light of a different hue is projected, the compositional colouring scheme will appear totally different. Brightly coloured substances reflect some degree of their near colour, a red transmitted will give off some red-orange as well as red-violet.

COLOUR DETECTION

Yellow and blue are detected by the eye at a wider peripheral degree than green or red. The eye may detect the form and mass of green or red, but the recognition of its colour will arrive to the eye later. This may be demonstrated by keeping the eye focused ahead and on one point in the distance. Move the colour from outside the peripheral vision towards the central vision. Yellow and blue are recognized more immediately than other colours. The colours green and orange may at first be perceived as yellow, whereas violet may be perceived initially as blue.

Exercise

Use watercolours for these exercises. Once complete, cut and paste into your sketchbook. Label all colours and their combinations clearly.

1. Produce mingling effects of colour by mixing with black, white and grey. Draw out a series of 5cm (2in) squares on to watercolour paper. Brush with water to wet the surface. Near the centre add a hue. While wet add to the surround a wash of black Indian ink. Let them mingle. Repeat this in other squares using different hues.
2. Repeat the above exercise using black watercolour paint instead of Indian ink. When both are dry, compare the differences between the same hues reacting to the different blacks.
3. Draw out another series of 5cm (2in) squares. Wet the paper and dab on a hue. While the square is still wet add a mid-grey made from mixing black and white paint. Let them mingle and blend. Repeat this using a choice of hues. Use the same grey mix each time. When dry note the apparent differences between the greys.
4. Choosing one or two examples of work already completed, apply the same coloured hue and grey over the top as a wash. When this dries, a layered effect of surprising quality and unique characteristics will be produced.

COMPLEMENTARY COLOURS

Complement means that which completes a deficiency. Complementary colours stand opposite one another on the colour wheel. The complementary colours for red, yellow and blue are green, violet and orange respectively. To test how close you may have come to finding the true complementary colour to a spectrum colour try out the following exercise.

Exercise

Paint a patch of a hue, when dry cut it into a square of approximately 1in (2.5cm). Place this on to a clean white page. Under daylight, stare for a good thirty seconds at this colour, then remove it from the page. Stare at the blank page. After a short time, you will see appear an illuminated square, with a colour influence. This after-image is the deficiency of colour rays which when combined with the original colour hue make white light. The colour image suggests at the pigment's complementary. The true complementary colour of a given hue when mixed together with it (in pigment) produces, when in equal parts, neutral grey. If the grey has a bias of colour towards any adjacent colour to the complementary on the colour wheel, then the complementary colours may not be true spectrum. For example, the complimentary colour to yellow is violet. If the neutral grey made from mixing these two colours is influenced by blue or red then the violet has too much of its adjacent colour in it.

Exercise

Draw out on watercolour paper a series of rows of five connected 2in (5cm) squares.

1. Wet one row of five squares with a brush. Place complimentary colours within each end square, use water to mingle the hues together across the inner three squares. Mingle red and green, yellow and violet, blue and orange, blue-green and red-orange, red-violet and yellow-green.
2. Wet another row of five squares, brush over with water and place at opposite ends a hue

107

and its near-complement. Use water to blend and mingle colour across the three inner squares. Near-complements are green and red-orange, blue and yellow-orange.

NOTES

1. With watercolour, adding white pigment raises the value of that colour, making it appear lighter. However, thinning the paint with water and brushing it over white paper lightens its value. The white of the page comes through the colour as does transmitted light through a substance, like light through a leaf.

2. Making colours brilliant requires the laying down of neutral grey as a surround. A neutral grey is nearly devoid of colour, and by contrast, the strength of the colour will be heightened.

3. The degree between light and dark where a colour comes to its full saturation or intensity is the spectrum value of the hue.

4. Adding white to lighten a blue, violet or purple weakens it. Yet through mixing in a little complementary, or a little neutral grey (as obtained through mixing complementary colours), or a little of its neighbouring colour on the wheel, the value is changed but not the intensity of the hue.

5. Bright lights reduce the intensity of colour. By over-saturating a substance with white light, other colour rays or spectrum hues are reflected back to the eye, making less pure the coloured substances.

6. When light hits obliquely, the reflection increases and produces a mirror effect, namely specular reflection. This specular reflection is all spectrum hues together, producing white light. The coloured substance therefore appears white.

7. In countries with bright light, effects of over-saturation upon opaque brilliant colours will harmonize or blend colours. This is through reflection of other spectrum hues along with the substance colour being reflected. This diminishes the intensity of colour.

8. In countries where grey predominates, opaque, brightly coloured substances appear intense in contrast to the neutral grey surround.

9. To the artist and designer, white and black pigment represent the brightest and darkest for that which is white and dark in nature. Paper will absorb half the light reflected upon it, a polished metal surface will reflect all the light. Design limitations are set by the brilliance of white fabric and black dye or paint. Design hints at nature's true spectrum.

10. Pure saturations or spectrum colours are rarely found in nature.

11. The neutral grey produced through mixing complementary colours has an illusive, shifting quality and is never wholly a grey devoid of colour, unlike mixings of black and white.

12. Mood and atmosphere through mixing complementary and near-complementary hues are richly varied. Shadows can successfully be suggested by using complementary colourings within the shadow. The Impressionist painters experimented with this characteristic of shadow. Black paint as shadow is lifeless, dull and flat.

13. Nature's autumn colours are discovered through complementary and near-complementary blendings. Note the earth tones in mixings of red and green, yellow and violet, orange and blue.

11 ARTIST'S MATERIALS

The surface that you choose to draw or paint on should act as an appropriate support for the medium used. Papers of various thicknesses offer differing supports, each being suited to a particular medium. It is disappointing when a surface lets you down technically. A poor foundation will ultimately fail to complement the work. Paint qualities range from children's watercolours to student paints, and artist quality paints. Student quality is affordable and ideal in most cases.

DRAWING BOARD

A necessary part of the studio, offering a portable surface to work on, and, when angled up, a perfect base to attach paper to and draw on. Use only masking tape to fix paper down unless you are stretching and attaching paper for watercolour work, in which case gum-backed paper tape should be used.

Drawing boards can be purchased from art supply shops, but it will prove a great deal less expensive to get something similar from the timber merchant, cut to your required size. A2, A1 and A0 are suitable sizes.

SCRAPBOOKS

Economical and available in large sizes, scrapbooks are ideal for pasting into and suitable for use as a handy reference on specific subjects. Accumulate cuttings from magazines, newspapers, periodicals and supplements. Begin collecting visual information on people, times, places, objects, nature, design, traditions and customs. Start your own library on hairstyles and facial hair, shoe design, hats and bags, gloves and umbrellas, lingerie, jewellery and spectacles. Archival scrapbooks become an excellent reference for the designer.

SKETCHBOOKS, PADS AND BLOCKS

A hardcover sketchbook, with college cartridge paper, is ideal for project work and daily sketching. The artist's sketchbook is available in various formats. Its portability and secure foundations serves the designer well. A sketchbook smaller than A4 is perhaps more suitable for the pocket, and convenient to jot down ideas and images while on the move.

Sketchbooks with heavy college cartridge or watercolour paper are suitable for combinations of drawing, collage, painting and ink work. When doing project work it is advisable to have one book for each project. Bound sketchbooks used for project work show process – ideas that have a beginning, middle and end. Large-scale sketchbooks encourage a bolder creative approach. Sketchbooks should reveal an inquisitive, searching, enquiring and inventive mind.

Tape- or spiral-bound sketch pads, in a large assortment of paper types, are available through many art and design outlets. The surface type and texture of the paper will differ according to the recommended medium, but it will be clearly stated, along with the weight.

In watercolour blocks, the paper is stacked and secured along its four edges with a water-resistant gum tape. After completion the painting should be set aside to dry still attached within the block. The taped edges keep the paper stretched and therefore consistently flat. Once dry the page can be torn out, revealing the next clean sheet beneath.

PAPERS

It is important to become familiar with different paper types and their weights. Feel the paper between the finger and thumb, note the thickness and surface texture, experiment with small sample sheets. Keep a logbook noting the various papers, their names and weights.

Paper starter packs, which offer a wide range of assorted paper types, are available through art material suppliers who will also be able to offer sound advice about an appropriate choice of paper for a specific purpose.

Surface Texture
There are three types of surface:

1. The smoothest surface is achieved through hot-pressing (HP), where the paper is pressed through sheets of metal. Cold-pressing (CP) is an alternative manufacturing process to achieve smooth surfaces.
2. NOT is a less-smooth surface. It may not have been pressed by a hot or cold press.

3. ROUGH is the least smooth. This is achieved by drying the sheets between rough felts and not through pressing. This paper is generally not hand-made.

Paper Weight
The weight of paper is measured in grams and referred to in grams per square metre (gsm). The greater the gsm, the thicker the paper will be. Paper may be bought by the sheet, the quire of 25 sheets, or by millbank which will vary in quantity from 50 to 1,000 sheets.

Different Types of Paper

College cartridge paper
Wood-free, available in natural white, weight 115gsm. Good quality and economical with a slight tooth to the surface. Particularly suitable for charcoal and pencil.

Heavy cartridge paper
Wood-free, weight 130–140gsm. Matt surface suitable for charcoal, pencil, pen and ink. Use heavyweight cartridge paper, weight 190–300gsm, for watercolour and printing processes.

Watercolour paper
A 100 per cent cotton rag paper, mould-made (m/m) with a gelatine size. Manufactured acid-free. Internally stretched, resulting in a surface resistant to fibre lift. Lines will not become feathered when pen and ink is used. Surface stands up to multiple erasures when using pencil and charcoal. Very stable with little or no distortion when soaking or applying heavy washes. Often produced with a deckled edge. Available in HP, NOT or Rough. Weight 150–640gsm.

Note: To stretch watercolour paper on to a board, first soak the paper in a bath of water until completely wet. Drain off excess water, then lay it out flat on to a smooth wooden board. Sponge it down flat with light pressure. Fix it to the board using extra-wide, gum-backed paper tape. Run a wet sponge across the tape surface, then flip it over and apply to the edge – the tape should straddle evenly the paper and board. Set aside to dry thoroughly. If using washes of colour use a minimum paper weight of 160gsm.

Pastel paper
A uniquely surfaced paper for the application of pastels or for printing. The tooth serves to hold the pastel. These papers are available in a wide range of colour tints, which may be either warm or cool in character. Darker tones will act as a stronger contrast. The tint shows through the applied pastel: this can offer an emphasis of colour, which integrates the work into a whole. Check that the paper is light fast – the better quality tint papers do not fade under light. For pastel or drawing work, use 90–100gsm.

Tissue paper
Available in a good range of colours, ideal for collage and scale-figure model making, used as an application to model surfaces to create fine-textured surfaces.

Layout paper
An ideal see-through paper for graphic and design work. Weight 45gsm plus.

Marker paper
Extra white non-bleed, transparent paper for markers, coated to be streak-free. Weight 70gsm.

Tracing paper
A light to heavyweight paper for artwork layover. Weight 60gsm plus.

Acetate sheeting
A clear and protective overlay. Permanent markers will dry to streak free.

Tri-Acetate
A specialist acetate sheeting on the roll, suitable for mixed media applications.

Stencil/oiled manilla paper
A thick paper manufactured for stencil work. The paper is treated with vegetable oil making it resistant to water. Size 762x508mm.

BOARDS

Mount board
Suitable for model-making and mounting or framing costume drawings for presentation. Available in white or coloured on one side. A light board of 1,000 microns or 725gsm.

Museum board
Acid-free, so suitable for conservation work, with solid colour throughout. A heavy board of 1,500–2,200 microns. When framing, always use acid-free boards to mount the drawings. Acid-free board, when ageing, does not affect drawing paper either through discolouring or deterioration.

Foam board or foam core
A double layer of lightweight white or black card with a thin layer of foam sandwiched between, used as a presentation base for drawings. Sizes 3, 5 and 10mm.

PAINTS AND INKS

Colour Pigment
Available in powder form, to which agents are added for binding. Early binding methods involved the use of sizing materials like honey, gum or egg. Cold-pressed linseed oil mixed with

111

pigment produces oil paint. Egg yoke and linseed oil mixed with pigment produces tempera. Gums, honey, glycerine, ox gall and pigment produce watercolour. Resin compounds mixed with water and pigment produce acrylic.

Acrylic

Acrylic, polymer-based paints have a binding medium of minute solid particles of plastic resin suspended in water. Acrylic paint comes in a wide colour range. Acrylics dry rapidly and are water insoluble when dry. They are of a flexible nature and do not yellow with age. The result is a permanent, durable plastic paint film. There is a fluid range, made with pigment not dye, offering strong colour with thin

---

Note

Brushes must never be left to rest with acrylic paint in the bristle, they need to be kept wet at all times, wash thoroughly with soap and cleanwater.

Initially purchase spectrum colour hues. To make a colour wheel and to set up your first paint-box, choose the pure saturations or brilliant hues. These represent the true pure primary and secondary colours known as spectrums (see page 105). Buy the mixed colours, which are blends of spectrum colours, at a later date. Avoid too elaborate a pre-mixed range initially. With an understanding of the colour wheel, you may prefer to mix colours yourself, rather than using mixed colours from a commercial range.

If the screw top of the tube is left off for extended periods, the paint will dry hard. Although this should be avoided, the paint will become liquid again when mixed with water.

---

consistencies, like Indian ink. The disadvantage for costume rendering and model making is in their rapid drying time which does not allow for easy blending of colour, and once dry they become insoluble.

Watercolour

Watercolour has a moisturising agent so even if left standing unused for months it will immediately become fluid when water is added. The binding agent ensures that the pigment is dispersed evenly. The established brand names produce high-quality paints in an excellent range of colours. Binding agents or gums may include honey and gum arabic. Watercolour paint contains no opacifiers and are therefore translucent. Watercolour is available in tubes as a liquid paste or in pans as dried cakes. The pans have dehydrating ingredients acting as a moisturiser. Pans can be bought separately, per colour choice. Metal or lightweight plastic boxes are available in an assortment of sizes to house the pans. The paint-box becomes a treasured life-long companion.

Gouache

Gouache is a water-soluble, opaque paint that remains soluble when dry. Sold in tubes and available in a wide range of colours including gold and silver, gouache produces a solid, opaque finish that covers the paper ground colour, and has a good mass tone. The medium is gum arabic – a dextrine solution in water. Gouache will dilute to a wash. Use with a sable, bristle or nylon brush. Gouache is suitable for applying to paper, board, or watercolour blocks, with or without a gesso or prepared size ground. An excellent paint for all designer tasks – costume sketching, renderings and set model work.

Inks

Inks are available in a range of qualities and prices. The traditional ink has a shellac medium as a base, which dries to a water resistant, satin-like gloss film. The white and black Indian inks are based on light-fast pigments, the colour is a soluble dye. It is preferable to dilute with distilled water. Dye inks are said to be not as light-fast as pigment-based inks.

ARTIST'S INSTRUMENTS

Pencils

Graphite pencils range from the very hard F-, hard H-, through to the very soft B-range. They are numbered to denote degrees of softness within each range. 2B is less soft (or less black) than 6B. 2H is less hard than 5H. The F-range is more suited to drafting and technical drawing. The H, HB, B, 2B through to 6B ranges are well liked for drawing.

The pencil is available in many ranges and types such as carbon pencils with French chalk mixed in with the lead (2H–3B). Traditional drawing pencils are available in white, sanguine and sepia; flat or round; and water-soluble versions.

Coloured pencils

Coloured pencils are available in a wide range of colours and qualities. They may be of a waxy composition, water-soluble, or pastel in nature. The preferred surface is a smooth paper – avoid grained or heavy-textured papers.

A mark made by a watercolour pencil can be brushed over with water, this produces a softened wash of colour. A wet brush over two colours blends or mingles colour. Dip the tip of the watercolour pencil in water then draw, the line produced is strong in its intensity of colour. Wax-based crayons repel water and ink washes.

Erasers

1. Natural rubber for pencil.
2. Putty art eraser for soft pencil, charcoal and pastel work.

Chalk

Conte is a French chalk, compressed into firm sticks. Like chalk, it is soft and does not retain a sharpened point for long. It produces a soft, translucent colour field when gently rubbed across paper. You can apply other mediums over such a ground: pencil, ink or paints. Ingres and textured, colour-tinted pastel papers are designed for pastel and chalk use. These finely textured papers grip the chalk within its textured recesses, the surface texture (or tooth) retains some of its original colour. It is possible to suggest form with surface light reflection by letting the white of the page highlight through the pastel. The white tooth suggests a broken light effect, it creates an atmosphere of light upon surfaces of form.

Charcoal

Available in soft birch willow, as compressed charcoal sticks, or in the pencil format with a range of densities.

Dip-pens

Pen drawings can successfully explore form either as a solid line drawing or when the line searches or seeks to discover form through an accumulation of related lines. In the first instance, think of the work of Piccasso and Matisse; in the latter, observe Giacometti. Both approaches are worth experimenting with. Do not be afraid to draw over your first observations. Working through to discovery may entail a building up of the form.

Pen drawing with black ink is bold and has a dynamic quality. Coloured drawing inks are also available. You may wish to sketch out the observed form with a lighter toned ink, then proceed with a darker ink thereafter. Try using coloured inks on coloured papers. Try to keep the pen and its line flowing through the entire form of the figure. This may mean sweeping lines that search out the overall position or posture first.

113

Felt-tip pens
The use of felt-tip pens can be disappointing due to their even line characteristics. The dip-pen offers a more expressive line. There are, however, felt-tip pens that have bevelled points which produce a more calligraphic quality line.

Brushes

Art shops generally offer three categories of brush: economical, studio, and professional. Cheap brushes can prove expensive in the long run. They soon lose their shape, hair or bristles. Quality artist's brushes are a good investment if properly cared for. It cannot be emphasized enough how much care needs to be bestowed upon the artist's brush. It is both painful and a shame to lose a good brush through neglect.

Hog bristle brush
Taken from hogs (a Chinese breed of long-haired pig). Most suitable for oil painting and professional brushes. The strong broad root of the bristle lends itself to being fixed into the brush. A strong, durable hair, the end of which forks into three to create a soft painting brush. Available in flat or round shaped brush ends.

Sable brush
Taken from the Russian sable, this watercolour brush is of exceptional quality. Available in kolinski, red or black sable, the brushes are hand made with excellent spring to the hair. Suitable for oil, watercolour or acrylic paints. With the price being high for sable brushes, it is particularly important that the brush is properly cared for.

Squirrel or squirrel and synthetic mixed hairbrush
Good quality watercolour brush, ideal for laying in washes.

Watercolour synthetic and nylon brush
A good range in shape and grade for the student or beginner.

Glue/paste brush
A round bristle brush with a specially designed clamp and plug at the base of the hairs suitable for applying pastes, glues and gesso.

Stencilling brush
Black or white bristle brush, round with a flat end for stippling against the paper flat on to its surface.

When using brush and ink or paint the outcome of a drawing is of a less tentative nature. Laying in washes of ink encourages a search for mass and volume through light and shade. Shading or blocking in shadow helps create more solid form. A wash of ink or paint to suggest form followed on by a dip-pen drawing produces most effective results. Note the drawings of Rembrandt, Schiele, Piranesi, Constable and Roualt.

SIZING

Rabbit skin glue
A natural sizing in crystal form, to be soaked in water and heated through on a double boiler.

Sizing is used as a primer for canvas, or a medium to be mixed with pigments. This traditional medium is also used when painting with oil colours. Sizing protects the canvas from the oxidizing effects of linseed oil found in oil paints and grounds.

Prepared size
A gelatine sizing used to reduce the absorbency of paper, board and lightweight textiles. It is applied with a brush and flows more easily when its container is warmed in a pan of hot water for a few minutes.

Gesso
A white or off-white opaque sizing, used as a primer for paper, card, board or masonry. Suitable for acrylic, gouache, oil pastel and paint applications, gesso gives a matt finish with a porous tooth surface. Gesso is available from sculpture shops either pre-mixed or as a powder, which should be mixed with water and a drop of linseed oil. The surface should be finely sanded after the first application to create a glass-like smoothness. Tempera painting is done on board with gesso as the ground.

Glues/Adhesives

PVA (Poly Vinyl Acetate)
The adhesive content of the glue is referred to as 'solids'. This water-based glue seems transparent when dry, giving a glaze or varnish finish that is waterproof. Depending on the solids content, the strength of the glue will range from 'general purpose' to a durable and dependable adhesive for bonding wood. General purpose PVA is suitable for hardboard, mount board, paper and other absorbent surfaces.
Starch paste
Suitable for all paper work and for papier mache.

Gum mucilage
Suitable for all paper work and for board, washes out without staining.

Aerosol spray adhesive
Suitable for bonding most common materials – paper, board, plastics, fabrics. Some makes are even suitable for polystyrene and foam.

Other Accessories

Aquapasto
A translucent gum jelly, miscible with water. It adds an impasto effect to watercolour. This effect gives body to the paint. Suitable for watercolour.

Acrylic modelling paste
Either sold as light or heavy putty, used to build up special effects in texture. Can be either mixed with acrylic or painted upon once dry.

Note

Wash out glue spreaders and brushes immediately after use by flushing first with cold water then warm water and soap. Pay particular attention to cleaning the roots of brushes out thoroughly. Any clothing that comes into contact with PVA needs to be washed immediately. It is advisable to wear an apron when using acrylic paints and PVA-based glues. PVA does not wash out once dry.

Some manufacturers create aerosols that do not contribute to ozone depletion. Because they contain petroleum distillates, the vapour may be harmful. Vapours also may ignite explosively. Always read the safety instructions prior to purchase and before use.

Art masking fluid
A rubber latex waterproof film, available with or without pigment, which protects areas from colour applied in broad washes. It may be removed with an eraser or peeled off.

Gum arabic
A natural gum and water preservative. Increases gloss and transparency. It is the primary watercolour binder.

Watercolour medium
A pale-coloured gum solution to improve flow of watercolours.

Fixative
Quick-drying, elastic, colourless and non-yellowing. Suitable for pastel, charcoal, pencil and chalk. Sold in aerosols and in bottles.

Acrylic resin fixative
Ideal for creating a waterproof seal to watercolour, Indian ink and tempera.

Low-odour fixative
A popular fixative for pastel, crayon or charcoal.

Pure turpentine
Used for reducing the consistency of oil colours and mediums. Turpentine and white spirit may be used to clean brushes, palettes and tools which come in contact with the oil base.

Colour spray paints
Artist and craft aerosol sprays come in a wide range of colours which can be applied to paper, card and board. Some are suitable for plastic, polystyrene, metal, wood and leather, and offer a water- and weather-resistant protective coating. The craft sprays may be less toxic and not water resistant. Check the aerosol is CFC free and always read the label thoroughly prior to purchase and before using. Always spray in a well-ventilated area and keep out of reach of children.

CLEANING UP

Oil paint
When using any oil-based paint, the brush needs a continued flushing out with white spirit or turpentine to release the pigment and binders. The oils and pigment become caught up right to the neck of the bristle, where it joins the metal ferrule. After flushing out, the bristle brush should be washed out thoroughly with household washing-up liquid or soap and plenty of warm water. A gentle yet firm massage is all that is necessary when cleaning brushes, but it must work its way into the base of the hairs. Keep oil paintbrushes away from watercolour brushes.

Acrylic paint
Brushes need immediate attention after use. They must be thoroughly washed out to expel all paint and the resin binder. After several good rinses, wash out with washing-up liquid or soap, gently squeeze dry with the fingers, carefully shaping the hair back towards its manufactured shape.

Watercolour or gouache
While painting with watercolour or gouache, the brush need not necessarily be rinsed with water. However at the end of the work session it will need a thorough yet gentle flushing out, followed by a wash using washing-up liquid or soap. Gently squeeze the water out with your fingers and reshape the hair into its manufactured shape. Place brush and ferrule carefully into the narrow plastic tube supplied for storage.

Brush holder/washer

This metal device is available commercially. The base container is for either turpentine or water, suspended above the base is a coil spring or metal spiral. The brush handle slides between the spring coils, leaving the brush's bristle dangling within the base liquid solution. An ideal accessory.

MIXING MEDIA

Experimenting with mixed media on differing surfaces will expand your creative and expressive horizons extensively. Be encouraged to explore the relationships that develop through alternative mark making. History offers exciting examples of artists expressing themselves through using mixed media. The variety of paper surfaces and texture adds to the expression. Take time to look through drawing and painting books, note the artist's medium and paper or other surface details.

Examples of Mixed Media

- Pencil and watercolour.
- Pencil and ink.
- Pencil and gouache.
- Pen and white ink on dark-coloured or black paper.
- Charcoal over dry watercolour that is then rubbed over in part with a putty eraser.
- Oil pastel over a painted acrylic coloured ground.
- Conte pencil over a painted acrylic coloured ground.
- Watercolour, black chalk and gouache.
- Pencil, watercolour, gouache and gum mucilage.
- Watercolour, gouache, conte and pastel.
- Oil paint, turpentine and oil pastel.
- Pen and ink, watercolour, gouache and chalk.
- Pastel pencils and watercolour.
- Charcoal, watercolour, pastel, ink and collage.
- Candle wax as a drawing instrument, washes of watercolour or washes of ink.
- Oil pastels with brushings of turpentine to effectively blend colour.
- Oil pastel and ink.

12 DRAWING, PAINTING AND THE THREE DIMENSIONAL

Theatre work involves many different drawing skills: architectural drawings representing the theatre space and the acting area, along with its designed scenery; a storyboard which shows a visual sequence of events and various focal points; artist's renderings which present impressions of scenes with attention to characters in a space with lighting; costume character sketches describing all clothing and accessories; and measured or scale drawings and sketches for furniture, properties and set dressing.

DRAWING

Drawing is a way of seeing things. Yet before one can 'see', one must, in the first instance, use the mind to think. Before the act of drawing, one sees or observes, but to see something in the mind's eye, is the act of using the mind to think. In simple terms: think, visualize, then draw.

Nature
The most informative teacher for drawing is nature. Through her relationships, and in her truths the designer and artist looks for explanations of the truth. Any study of nature through drawing, painting and sculpture, is a study of truth. However, nature does not come to you, you must want and need to reach out.

Process
The act of drawing becomes a mental exercise with the results showing process and attitude. The hand becomes a mere instrument

An extraordinarily delightful study for Mrs Foresight. Love For Love. *Designer: Ann Curtis. Stratford Festival Theatre*

118

Student line drawing. One continuous line, drawn without looking at the page, only at the sitter. Julie. Dali-Costume Design at Central St. Martins

controlled by the mind. Develop respect for what your mind has to say, and develop a trust by training your hand to faithfully serve the mind. Through exercise and practice, a bond will develop between the mind 'seeing' and drawing, and the outcome reveals these relationships.

Drawing involves active enquiry. Drawing, painting and sculpture are forms of searching. Mark-making develops into a language. And with it is conveyed idea, thought, observation, imagination, and emotion. Drawing from life becomes an active engagement, and the drawing becomes a record of the level of engagement or a representation of the act of exploration. The exploration may show: a build up of spatial relationships; enquiry into

Student line drawing. One continuous line.

lines of growth and growth patterns; a search for pure form through line, light and shade; a search of relationship through texture; a sense of achieving compositional order.

Characteristics of Drawing

The expressive characteristics of drawing are to be found in its elements. These are line, texture, form, and values of light and dark. Design employs these elements with the addition of colour to investigate, interpret, and express. Through using the materials and mediums readily available for drawing and painting, the designer approaches problem solving on familiar ground. The fine arts and graphic design show rich examples of media serving to communicate and express. Through the act of drawing, we make ourselves articulate: we communicate.

Approach

Begin by finding things to draw that really interest you. When something captures your interest it captures your imagination as well. Like most things that are enjoyable, having sufficient time is important. Take your time while drawing, and don't try too hard. Straining to draw is counter-productive. Enjoy the process.

Drawing In One Continuous Line

Exercise: The Face

This method of drawing is remarkably useful. With practice, the results prove honest and surprisingly expressive. It also becomes easier to do with time. This exercise, by its very nature, assists in the development of co-ordination between eye and hand. Be sure never to look at the page throughout the exercise.

Seat yourself opposite someone at a table, so you face them front on. Place squarely before you, an A4 sheet of paper, in a portrait position, and take in hand a soft-leaded 2B pencil. Place the pencil tip at the page centre, then stare at the face opposite. Fix your eyes on one central feature, observing it well. Now let your eye, very slowly, travel across the contour and plane of the face. It may be of some help initially to imagine yourself the size of the tip of the pencil, pushing a large ball across the surface. Where the eye travels, the hand follows. They move in unison. The line is a record of the eye's journey. It is very important not to remove the pencil tip from the page, and to avoid allowing the eye to dart about. Explore the facial regions slowly: look with interest, and enjoy the individual features which are particular to this character. Avoid generalizations, this is where the line makes a sweeping gesture for a contour. The features should not be looked at too superficially. Draw for two or three minutes.

The results should portray a face, created with one continuous line, with a beginning and an end. The slight distortion and measure of exaggeration should be a pleasant and welcome surprise. There is another surprising aspect in these drawings, which should capture your attention and interest, and this is especially true when the pupils of the eye are included. The resulting drawings portray character.

After completing several such studies, set them alongside each other, and compare them. It is particularly constructive to discuss them with someone. Establish, between you, which character traits the drawings show. Any such criticism is now directed to the drawn image, we are not here discussing the sitter or model. What is of interest is what the drawing says, through character of line,

Student line drawing, imagining the sitter to be of royal blood. Drawn without looking at the page.

One continuous line. Alessandro Costantino

Student line drawing.
One continuous line. Henriett Fisher

quality of line, and the impression it makes as a whole image. Aspects that you both agree on as being common to the character will prove to be of importance. Discuss why you both happened to agree on these subjective observations of character: what makes you agree the character appears of a particular age, of a vibrant or reserved character, seeming naive or of some complexity. The answers are revealing and informative. Understanding what makes the drawing so expressive helps develop your own attitude when picking up paper and pencil to do further studies. Do not discard these as bad or inferior drawings.

One continuous line. *Student work. Dali-Costume Design at Central St. Martins*

121

Exercise: The Figure

Now take the previous exercise a stage further. Sit opposite someone who is sitting some 4m (13ft) away. Follow the same rules as before: do not look down at the page, study the form from head to toe, and examine the form in its entirety. You may wish to include part of the chair. Draw for two to three minutes. A keen model may be happy to both sit for longer periods or stand in various simple poses. Avoid labouring in one area for too long, instead keep a flow to your observations, allowing the eye to travel from one area into another, and make connections. With the figure at a greater distance from the eye, the measure of scrutiny or observation will be less detailed than over a small area such as the face.

Look for other opportunities that arise which offer the perfect model. People often sit or stand still for long periods while waiting for the bus, in cafes and restaurants, in conversation on the street and in shops, while they rest, watch television or sleep. Carry an A5 or A4 sketchbook with you at all times. The smaller sketchbook may help you remain unnoticed. These studies become a record of character in place and time. Note time and place, along with any written information to support the character and situation you feel relevant.

A recurring mistake in figure drawing is a failure to keep the figure on the page. Increasing the paper size is not the answer. It is good practice to set down boundaries or limitations for the head and feet by drawing a horizontal line near the top of the page and another parallel at the base of the page. This establishes a limitation to work within. Perhaps sketch in a broad oval or round shape, within which you will aim to work. After some practice, these preliminary construction lines are unnecessary.

Keeping the figure within the page dimensions, adding expressive bold lines and washes of ink to slightly exaggerate character. Too Clever By Half. *Arts Educational*

NAME _____

PLAY _____

CHARACTER _____

DATE _____

> Tie string around natural waist.
> Measurements to the floor are taken without shoes

HEIGHT ____   WEIGHT _____

NECK(base of throat) _____

CHEST/BUST ____ DIAPHRAGM ____ WAIST ____

UPPER HIP(approx.5" below waist) _____

LOWER HIP(full measure across seat)_____

ACROSS CHEST(armhole to armhole) _____

BUST POINT to BUST POINT (B.P.) _____

ACROSS BACK(armhole to armhole) _____

FRONT WAIST(base of neck to waist) _____

CENTRE SHOULDER to BUST POINT _____

CENTRE SHOULDER to WAIST _____

BACK WAIST (nape to waist) _____

NAPE to FLOOR _____

SIDE WAIST to BEND of KNEE _____ to FLOOR _____ INSEAM_____

GIRTH (front waist through crotch to back waist) _____

THIGH _____ BASE of KNEE _____ CALF _____ ANKLE _____

(WOMEN)FRONT WAIST to base of KNEE (skirt length)_____

SHOULDER (base of neck @ side to 'natural seam') _____

NAPE to POINT OF SHOULDER _____ to ELBOW _____ to WRIST _____

INSIDE ARM (armpit to wrist) _____ UNDERARM to WAIST _____

BICEP _____ ELBOW _____ FOREARM _____ WRIST _____

HAT ____ GLOVE ____ GARMENT ___ RING ____ SHOES ___ BRA ___ TIGHTS ___ PIERCED EARS?___

ALLERGIES/SPECIAL NOTES_____

---

                *   WIG & MILINARY MEASUREMENTS   *

HEAD CIRCUMFERENCE _____ HAIRLINE CIRCUMFERENCE _____ TEMPLE to TEMPLE _____

NAPE to HAIRLINE _____ EAR to EAR _____ EAR to NAPE _____ ACROSS NAPE _____

Actor measurement page.

Draw Yourself

Exercise
Using a full-length mirror, strip off to your underclothes and draw yourself standing. You may need to set up an easel, or alternatively position yourself with the drawing attached to a wall at your side. You can easily draw up to an arm's length away from the paper.

1. Note points of alignment for the joints and main parts of the body such as where your thigh and hand meet (arm extended along the side of the body).
2. Note the mid-point of the body between top of the head and toes.
3. Where the elbow meets the waist, note its position to the belly button.
4. Form a fist, bend your elbow so the fist and shoulder are side by side, note the alignments and lengths of the parts.
5. Bend the elbow, place the forearm horizontally across the front of your stomach, note the length of the forearm and compare to the width of the body.
6. Bend the knee by pulling the heel up to the bottom, note the measure of the parts.
7. Note the position of where the breast aligns between the elbow and shoulder.

Now turn sideways to the mirror.
1. Look at where the top and base of your bottom aligns with the waist, hip, thigh, and belly button.
2. Imagine a vertical line through the middle of the body, note the mass to either side. How much forward is your head of this line? How far back do the shoulders sit? Is the pelvis forward or backwards of the line? What shape has the spine? Does the stomach drop down and forward or is it pulled up and backwards?

Become familiar with your own figure, its shape and proportions. Study yourself seated before the mirror from a variety of angles. Vary the directional lighting angles so to produce differing effects that add dimension to feature through side lighting.

COSTUME DRAWINGS

Actors' Measurements
The wardrobe department will supply you with actors' measurements. The information is useful for imagining what you will start with, as well as for comparison between characters within a scene. Relationships are concerned with the physical contrast and complement of one form to another. Setting out to highlight and heighten these character differences begins with contemplating the basic nude form of the actor.

The Nude
In costume design, the figure's shape and proportioning is an all-important part of their character. When making first impressions of a character, it is useful to imagine and draw him or her nude. The mass, weight and volume of character can be more honestly explored through the basic nude shape. It is an entertaining and constructive way into defining character. These impressions, especially when characters are drawn alongside one another, better describe character through such basic contrasts and comparisons. When finished costume drawings are handed over, one of the first questions the wardrobe mistress will ask is what the character is wearing underneath. Wardrobe asks this, knowing the actor's measurements. So the question is more about aspects of padding, building up and constraining which take place under the clothes. Drawing a character nude is therefore a parallel way to looking at what padding,

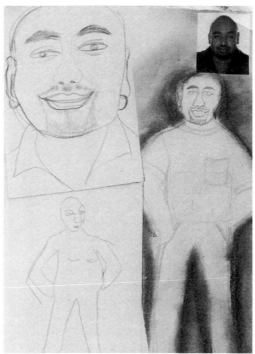

Taking an anonymous photograph of a face, the character was imagined as having a life history. A portrait drawing was made from studying the photograph, not looking at the page. With eyes closed, the nude figure was imagined. A suggestion of clothing was then drawn. Henriett Fisher

caging and corseting would have to be applied to the actor's own measurements. The approach proves more honest.

Social Influence

Character silhouette is developed through thinking about etiquette and manner which coincides with period and class attitudes. Period dress is always in some form complemented by etiquette. Poise may be as much a result of the constraints of fashion as social influences. Attitudes that coincide with fashion reflect attitude in a social context. The investigation into period dress is really an investigation into the influences that shape it, with marked distinctions between various social groups.

These distinctions may reveal themselves through freedom or restriction of movement in dress. The sense of being practical or of being impractical may also be important for differentiating where people stand in society.

Poise

Period dress can present an actor with many problems. Heel height alone affects the actor's poise, balance and movement. Costume drawings need to appreciate and express a measure of these elements. It may come across in the twist of the body and angle of the head to the shoulders, in the delicate nature of the shoe design and the poise of the legs and feet. When drawing up these aspects of character, it may be particularly helpful to stand and adopt these manners for yourself. Act out the attitude and note the alignments or twists of the body which shape themselves into becoming an expression of character.

Character Gesture and Pose

Exercise
Think of an attitude or opinion about something or someone. Consider arrogance, loathing or disdain, desire or lust, jealousy or envy. Then imagine the character. Stand up and act it out, giving over to strong feelings about it. Consider what makes you feel like this, focus on the cause, is it your wealth and independence, your obsessive nature, being slightly mad, or a feeling of misfortune? Imagine someone being at the receiving end of your attitude.

Use all the body, expressing the character from the top of the head through to the tips of your toes and fingers. Move about and act it out, consider how onlookers see you from every angle. Be expressive and exaggerate for dramatic impact. Feel the shape of the back, its twist; the tilt of the head and the position of the head to the shoulders. How are your legs positioned and feet angled? How is your balance distributed? What are the proud elements of the body? Do you walk lightly or with solid placement of the feet? What are the arms and hands saying? Close your eyes and get into character.

Now sit at the desk with A4 college cartridge and a soft pencil. Close your eyes and imagine the character. Keeping the eyes closed, draw the figure as you felt it. Use one continuous line, do not lift the pencil point and let the line express a character, which may be lyrical or delicate, aggressive or bold, timid or neurotic in nature. Draw out all the figure, from head to toe. Take on a viewpoint that best captures the expressive gesture. The character is very interesting – be sure that the drawing shows this. Think about the proportions, the shape, form and silhouette, together with pattern and texture.

Metaphor and Simile

Exercise
Think of a character as being something other than what they appear to be – maybe a sparrow, a vulture, a walrus; a brittle twig, a rose bush, a gilded lily; like a trumpet sounding or an out of tune violin; like a golden sunset or a tempestuous sea. Consider your own family and friends for this exercise. Use a scrapbook to collect a series of images which describe them and note the relevance of the images. Perhaps it is the way in which they march along or drag their feet; the rapid, darting manner of the head; or the whole gentle shift and flow of body mass which makes you think of a walrus. Perhaps they appear to have several characteristics which are in opposition to one another – one being gentle, the next ferocious. Collage these images together so the outcome is a relation of two odd parts. Back up your visual study with written descriptions of their character.

Anatomy

Costume drawings need not be exercises in anatomically correct figures. Labouring over accurate anatomical structure may not prove constructive if it gets in the way of expressing character first. A balance of measured proportioning is appropriate, but more importance should be given to character traits, manners, attitude and the eccentricities which go with each.

How to Achieve Reasonable Proportions

The human figure varies greatly: people come in all shapes and sizes. Schools of figurative art study the model with a relentlessly critical, yet passionate eye. Students are trained to

An imagined character, showing itself as lively through the quality of line. One continuous line. Drawing done with eyes closed.
Uta Gruber-Ballehr

Collage for an imagined extrovert character.
Patricia Ward

proportion out the figure. They make measurements by using the hand and eye together. Some of these techniques are useful. Life drawing classes are of great value to the designer, and most design schools incorporate life drawing into the curriculum.

Exercise: The Generalized Approach
1. The body, standing and facing forward, can be divided up into equal measured sections. The head height serves as one measurement, from the top of the head to under the jaw or chin. The body is divided into eight sections with each section being the same measurement as the head. Draw an oval or circle at the top of the page, representing the head. Repeat this measurement beneath, seven times more. Two head measurements is the location of

the nipples. Three heads locate the waist and elbows. Four heads locate the pelvis region or top part of the groin. Five heads locate the mid-thigh and tips of fingers. Six heads locate the lower knee. Seven heads locate the lower calf. This generalized formula for proportions helps in the initial stages of plotting out the figure.

Exercise: The Studied Approach
This method is useful when drawing from life. The model should be some 4m (13ft) away from you. Hold a pencil upright as if it were a lollipop stick. Fully extend your arm in front of you and close one eye, lining up the tip of the pencil with the top of the head. Now position the top edge of your thumb along the vertical shaft, so it is in line with the lower chin. This measure acts as the guide to locating other

127

***Six-inch-high wire, plastercine and tissue
paper figure.***
Based on a collage. Patricia Ward

points of the body as you lower your extended
hand down over the figure. Keep the arm fully
extended and slowly lower the tip of the pencil
to align with the bottom of the chin. Note
what the top of the thumb now aligns with.
Continue lowering the pencil tip, and note
these continued alignments.

Make notation on the drawing page by first
choosing a measure for the head (one which
when added to approximately seven more will
fit the page). All measurements on the page are
in relation to the head measurement. The
measurement made while looking at the model
will be in a different scale. When you refer back
to the model, start again with a fully extended
arm, locate the top of the head with the pencil
tip, and the chin with the top of the thumb,
then work across the figure both vertically and

horizontally. Once the points of measured
alignment are recorded on the page, a more
freestyle drawing can be applied over these
registrations, and the result will be a well-
proportioned figure.

Figure Drawing

When sketching from life avoid drawing the
outline alone. Explore across the body, over
and around the form within, and use the
continuous line drawing technique to record
your observations. Discover the outer form by
working from the centre out. This way, the
internal forms and their proportions come
together to form the outline.

***Finding the form of character through
pulling it out of a haze of lines, and adding
watercolour washes for accent.***
*Actor Michael Loughnan as William Blake,
in* Blake

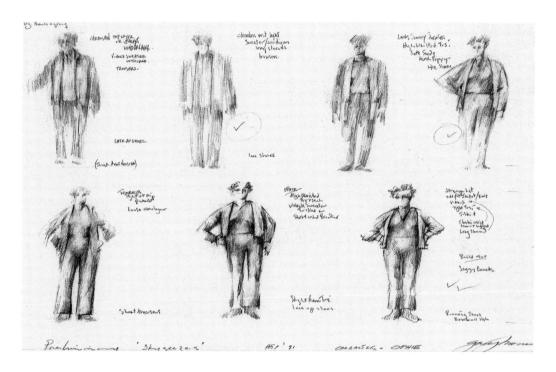

Searching for form through lifting the character out a void, each time adding slight shape to define. The final sketch is where the character's costume was headed.
Skygeezers. *Alberta Theatre Projects*

Studies of Draped Material

Exercise
By first making impressions of a character through drawing it nude, you better establish a figure which you then can begin to imagine as dressed. Drawing the clothing as a way to discover inner form is a more indirect approach. Making observations of fabric alone will help you to understand the very nature of fabric type. Studies of draped fabric make the eventual drawing of clothing easier.

Make separate studies by setting up a still life with various fabrics, one at a time. Drape material over the back of a chair or over a stable, secure object on a table. Focus the light from one direction, so the folds and recesses show shadow. The cross-lighting will also highlight the fabric's texture. Use a selection of pencils from 4H through to 6B on white paper. Make further studies using conté or coloured drawing chalks on tinted pastel paper, use white to highlight and add specular reflection.

Note: Drawings by Max Beckmann, Marc Chagall, Lucas Cranach the Younger, Daumier, Delacroix, Otto Dix, Durer, Hogarth, Hans Holbein the Younger, Edward Hopper, Ingres, Augustus Edwin John, Gustav Klimt, Oskar Kokoschka, Kaethe Kollwitz, Fernand Leger, Richard Lindner, Henri Matisse, Millet, Picasso, Rembrandt, Larry Rivers, Rouault, Egon Schiele, Watteau, and Andrew Wyeth.

CHARACTER STUDIES

Exercise
Select one of the following characters and use
it for the following exercises:
1. A 'writer' wearing his dressing gown.

'Darling how marvellous to see you. Why don't
you step in? Do have a wee gin and tonic with me!
I can't be seen drinking alone, and I always have
one at this time of the afternoon. I really could
not be getting on with writing without it ...The
novel darling! I'm a writer now, you must have
heard...Well, what was I saying? Yes, most of the
research comes from when I was in Chelsea – set
a few years back now...I write a column for a
London monthly, you know just to keep in
circulation, and to keep the drinks cabinet and
the rent in order, while I write the book. Well
actually I write about retro-collectibles, not
antiques, just bric-a-brac really, terribly boring
stuff, yet it's all the rage this retro. Anyway, the
PR parties for work are marvellous, lots of free
booze and chat. I hope to slip off to Tuscany, to
get away from it all, to get a grip on the novel, in
early September, less tourism and of course
cheaper flights. Well, actually I've only just
finished the book's introduction. Another drink?
You don't mind if I do?'

2. A beautiful young woman living with
   her fame

'It's all very demanding you know. The
filming is the easy bit – no honest, that part
comes so naturally to me. I can't seem to do
anything wrong in the eyes of the director.
They treat me like royalty. They give me
everything on a platter: the outfits, the
dinners, the chauffeur – it's fab, I love it! Not
a moments peace though, and no private life
I'll have you know. You try popping out at
any time of day or night, impossible! You've
got to dress like your last film and never
without make-up and hair looking front-
cover girl gorgeous. The next shoot is a real
blockbuster, we're off to the Cayman
Islands. It's likely to become part one of who
knows how many, imagine it! I'll be a
redhead, and to think I've always wanted to
be one. Excellent part, full of character, a
kind of rebel type, biker babe, action packed,
the supporting men are to die for, and there
is hardly enough leather on all of us to re-
dress a cow. I can handle it, just give me the
bike, I'll show you!'

3. The hip film maker

'Yeah man, well it's a kind of a film, off-beat
movie I'm making, see. We're shooting in
Soho, late night kind of stuff, just the one
camera. No man, no there's no script, no
actors, we're into tearing all that commercial
film making stuff wide apart. It's new
groundbreaking material, this is about going
big, see. Who knows if anyone has hit upon
this idea before. Man, it's like we're not exactly
set up as yet. Give me a break, things are going
to take time. Yeah, I've got some filling in to do
with a TV promo, and videos and stuff. Well
I'm not producing like, right now, its, you
know, the way in with behind the scenes
work. Check this out, check that out.
Mainstream cinema's so way out of touch, it's
like so uncool, so, you know! Those jerks with
power just close the door on us hip guys with
ideas. Just you wait man and see.'

4. A young lady in a soft, flowing summer
   dress, wearing a large brimmed hat, caught
   surprised by a sudden gust of wind.
5. A terrible, hideous old witch, enjoying an
   evil laugh while stirring her bubbling
   cauldron of rat stew.
6. A happy, fat chef, carrying a large tray
   heaped high with delicious desserts,

unaware that he is about to step on a sleeping cat.

7. An arrogant, pompous dandy. A man who pays an excessive amount of attention to himself, his style of dress, and to his immaculate and tidy manner. He is fully enjoying a laugh at someone else's expense. He is tall and very slim, yet his dress makes him look rather ridiculous. He stands elegantly posed with a silver-handled walking stick, he holds a cigarette and wears his chin rather too high for his own good. His little hat is balanced in a rather silly way on a lavishly styled wig.

Sketches Bordering On Caricature

Exercise

First, put yourself into the shoes of the character. Stand up and let your whole body relax. Think about the character's situation. Imagine the atmosphere surrounding him or her. Become that character, act it out, and concentrate on showing attitude in an expressive and dynamic way. If you do not wish to use one of the characters from the previous exercise you can invent your own. Think about who you are speaking to. Picture the setting and location furnishings. Imagine the smells, the textures, and quality of light and dark and how it hits your body. Move about, acting out a short scene. Feel the weight, mass and balance of the body.

Take an A3 sheet of cartridge paper and a soft B pencil or compressed charcoal in a pencil form. Stand over the drawing table rather than taking a seat. Begin with the overall shape from head to toe, so to create a shape to work in and around. Use a scribbling action to arrive at mass or volume. Focus on the balance and poise overall. Draw all parts connecting through to another. Keep the pencil moving and draw across the body shapes. Build up the drawing contour through internal scribbling.

Exercise

Take an A4 lightweight college cartridge paper and some soft charcoal or one colour of chalk or conté. This time aim to capture the gesture more expressively. Caricature the fat round stomach, the rounded shoulders, large sagging bottom, fat thighs and tiny feet. Caricature the elongated bony head, neck, shoulders and torso through to the stretched out limbs and big feet. Perhaps the figure's balance is precarious – capture it in motion. Work boldly and draw from the shoulder. Press firmer to add weight of character. The line needs to support the character traits.

Sketch in props while you draw the figure, not as an afterthought. Choose props which describe the character's interest. The 'writer', for example, may have a waste paper basket full of crumpled pages. Do several drawings, viewing the character from different angles.

Note. In both this and the following exercise, detail should be kept on the backburner. Avoid the finer details such as costume and distinctive facial features. Create an impression through silhouette. Make several studies which flesh out the character. Think of it as a lump of clay that you mould into a shape. Give it shadow through contrast of light and dark.

Exercise

Take a fine paintbrush, black ink or paint, A3 heavyweight college cartridge paper and a container of water. Position the paper to landscape (the length laying horizontal). Sketch out with the brush three poses for the character, viewed from different angles. Draw using a continuous brush stroke from head to toe, establish the balance and the figure's mass or volume. Use washes of colour to build up the shape and form. Washes serve as shadow, build up layers to imply weight.

131

Exercise

Pin your sketches up nearby and begin new drawings that are focused on clothing and dress detail. Draw, looking at the sketches you have already done as model forms to dress. Imagine the shape and fit of costume over the figure. Use pencil, ink, pastel and washes of colour.

THE THREE-DIMENSIONAL FIGURE

Exercise

Use your sketches from the above characters as reference. For this exercise you will need:
- soft, fine gauge wire suitable for modelling (available through hardware, DIY and garden shops)

Collage detail of the face by Anna Strobl.

- the plastic lid of a container (a yoghurt lid works well)
- modelling material or plastercine
- wire cutters
- needle nose pliers
- white tissue paper
- paper gum or paste
- fine-modelling tools
- masking tape

Poke four holes, the thickness of the wire, in the plastic lid. The holes should be 2.5cm (1in) apart, positioned to form a square at the centre of the lid. Cut two lengths of wire each 50cm (20in) long. Pass one wire through a hole until it is half-way through, bend it into a 'U'-shape and pass the end back through the hole in the diagonally opposite corner of the square. Pass the other wire through the other holes in the same way. Push the 'U'-bends against the base of the lid with the thumb, twist the long strands of wire together, a pair at a time, until tight. Using masking tape, fix the lid to a work table surface. The vertical wires should then be twisted and shaped into an armature for the boney structure of the figure. Make the figure stand approximately 15cm (6in) high. Twist in more lengths of wire where needed to add volume and mass to the internal structure or skeleton. Use needle nose pliers to tighten the twisted wire ends. The wire ends can be simply twisted round any part of the existing shape. Base the armature shape on the ink wash or charcoal drawings, and aim to copy the silhouette shape, emphasizing the balance and its proportions.

Add plastercine to the armature to flesh out the form, but avoid too solid a fill. Instead, flatten out pieces of the modelling material and lay over the armature like a skin. Cover all the wire. For the head, press in a thick lump of plastercine, especially across the face, so detailed modelling of features can be achieved later.

Scale wire, plastercine and tissue paper
figure, based on collage and drawings.
Left: Uta Gruber-Ballehr. Right: Anna Strobl.

Tear the tissue paper into stamp-size pieces. Apply the glue liberally to both sides and press it on to the plastercine. Cover the whole form except for the face and head. All hats, shoes and accessories should be made in the same way, with an outer layer of tissue and glue. Once dry, apply another layer, this time constructing more of the costume using the tissue paper.

Once built up and allowed to dry, work can begin on the face, adding the nose, ears, and indentations for eyes and mouth. You may wish to add thread or yarn for hair. When complete, brush over the whole sculpture with a slightly diluted wash of PVA or carpenter's wood glue. This seals and protects the materials: two coats are advisable. Allow to dry thoroughly before painting over.

This constructive exercise helps the designer consider the costumed figure in a three-dimensional form. Drawings based on observing the three-dimensional form then become all the more comprehensive through the knowledge of side and back views.

Exercise
1. Draw from nature, study plant stems and branches with leaves and berries. Collect pods, such as acorns attached to a sprig of oak leaves.
2. Pick fresh flowers, study them from different viewpoints, make line drawings and drawings made up of nothing but dots on the page. Study internal relationships which give form distinctive shapes. Take the flower apart, draw its parts separately.
3. Collect feathers, shells, and stones. Note the direction and texture produced through growth.
4. Draw collections of shoes, old and new.
5. Assemble crumpled paper bags, create a still life, and draw the folds, crevices, and characteristics.
6. Draw skeletons and dead insects.
7. Draw insects and animals both in captivity and in the wild.

Drawing In Three Dimensions

Here the drawing is concerned with the length, breath and width. The mass and form become sculptural in space. Discover the three dimensional through line, texture, light and shadow.

Exercise
1. Take a curved leaf and view it from an angle.

Unfinished 'Writer in a dressing gown'.
Sonia Tchatcko

Testing proportions with cut-out and painted scale figures against the dining room table in Three Sisters.
Designer: Debra Hanson.
Stratford Festival Theatre

Finished scale figures based on collage and drawings. Left: Salvo Manciagli.
Right: Emma Goodwin

Scale figures at 1:50 in wheelchairs, very fine detailed model pieces.
Designer: Alison Chitty

Use a continuous line drawing to explore its shape. Draw out its double-sided nature. Note the internal direction of growth. Dried leaves provide a variety of sculptured form, the leaves twist and turn in surprising ways.

2. Place a cup, saucer and teapot on the table, an arm's length away from you. Position the cup so you can see partially inside. Let your continuous line drawing roam around the surfaces in and outside. Make the lines dense and heavy where there is shadow.

3. Draw the same cup using only dots on the page. Use the same way of looking and a continuous line made from dots in a row and alongside one another. A soft pencil, ink dip-pen or felt tip will do. Cluster the dots close together where the areas are darker and further apart where the light is brightest against the form.

4. Draw rooms full of furniture. Use the continuous line technique without looking at the page. Paint out an impression of the same room using only washes of white to black paint or ink, this time observing form as light and dark masses.

5. Study all fruit and vegetable forms.

SHADING

Exercise

1 Shading is the gradation of tone from light to dark. Colour needs to be thought of in value from light to dark. Make a drawing or painting of a colourful still life, using only values of black through the greys to white. Consider the relative value of colour in gradations of grey. Photograph the still

Scale figure. Gypsy Taylor

'The Oscar winner'. Charlotte Crozier

'Femme fatale'. Parry Divania

The 'writer'. Charlotte Crozier

Scale figure and brush painted impressions of the Witch. Venetia Norris

life using black and white film. Compare the results.

1 Take an apple and place it so there is one light source hitting it. Draw out its contour first to establish shape. Using a harder pencil such as an H, shade the light tones in. As you progress into the mid-range shades change to an HB and when shading the darkest regions use a 2B. The direction of the shading lines may best go in the direction of the growth of the apple. The apple's expanding lines show direction of growth.

3 Cut a section or quarter out of the apple. Draw it in its parts. Note the bright value of the inner flesh compared to the light values on its surface. Peel the apple and draw its peel. Note the play of shadow on the coiling peel and the three-dimensional aspects of such an abstract form.

4 Mix a range of values from black to white using white and black ink or paint. Limit the values to white, pale grey, light grey, mid-grey, dark grey, very dark grey, and black. Paint studies of the apple and peel, cup and saucer, and the draped fabric.

5 Use an eraser as an instrument for drawing. Draw using soft pencil or charcoal, and at the same time mark-make

with the eraser. The eraser marks are considered equal in merit to the drawn line.

DRAWING FROM MEMORY

Draw from memory – trust yourself to remember accurately what is important about the character and situation. Allow vague impressions to surface on the page first, concentrate on form and silhouette and their proportioning. Build up the overall picture through a series of drawings. Let each attempt explore another facet of the character. Draw with the eyes closed. Draw a character in relation

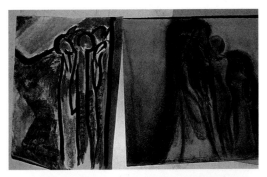

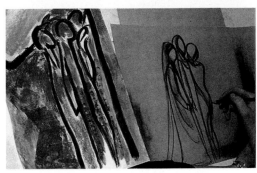

Using as inspiration a fragment from a Kandinsky painting, a bold painting was made, which was then developed into the charcoal and pastel drawing to the right, achieving a fleshing out of dress in an atmospheric setting. Maria Panei-Cabrita

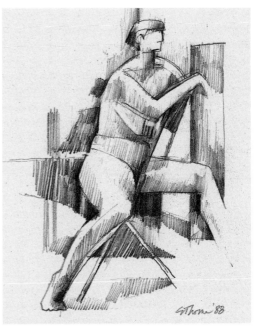

Life drawing.
Light values in pencil on tinted paper

Figure drawing from life.
Pencil on tinted paper

to another person: the differences will reveal something more about them. Use comparisons with animals to help you develop the image.

Commit objects, places and events to memory and rely on memory for the impressions. Draw from what you recall. Use the mind to 'see' and draw letting the hand be an instrument for the mind.

CHARACTERS IN LOCATION

When characters interact with location they reveal something more about themselves. We fit comfortably into some environments and less so in others. The play establishes character in location, which may act for or against the character.

Scale becomes an important issue: the proportions of the room in relation to the people and their numbers. Suggesting location

gives the character something to interact with, be it to create a relationship or to stand as a contrast to it. Within plays, characters are inextricably linked to the location and situation. When drawing and designing, it is of the utmost importance to consider character as part of location. The locations in the first instance are crucial for the playwright, and characters need the support of location to better emphasize and clarify their predicaments, plots, and directions. Location may only be atmosphere, yet that alone can serve to articulate the playwright's intentions.

STORYBOARD

The storyboard is presented through a series of drawings. These reveal how the acting space will be designed to serve the actor and support the play. The format is like stills or frames from

137

Figure drawing from life.

a film sequence. The viewpoint is that of the audience. The storyboard tells the story through movement and arrangement and tests design in terms of stage blocking.

It is important to focus both on individuals and groups, and consider the spatial dynamics of actors sharing the same space. Keep ideas relative to particular moments in the play and draw these moments in sequence using actor lines or page numbers as a reference. Draw characters in relation to minimal set and furnishings, and heighten lighting effect and shadow.

It is useful to include a sketch for a plan view alongside. This informs the director of proposed layouts. It should show details of entrance, exit, and movements across the acting space. Animate the play through focusing on the audience's point of view. It may prove helpful to draw as if looking down a

little upon the floor space, putting it into a slight perspective. This more clearly presents the layering of characters in space. With one location it is helpful to lightly sketch the setting in slight perspective, then photocopy many times, so one can draw over the copies.

For the actor and director, centre stage, downstage-left and downstage-right are always preferred areas on the proscenium stage. The dynamics are different on thrust, in-the-round, traverse, or arena stages. Use the storyboard as a stepping stone to better understand the differences. This approach proves useful and constructive in moving action forward towards an end, as well as establishing the actors' action and arrangement for the proper focus that a scene requires.

Characters paired together on the same page using one continuous line.
Ballpoint pen on ingre-tinted pastel paper

The closer the audience is (overall) the less 'theatrical' (in the sense of broad strokes) you have to be, or can be. The proscenium places you at a distance from the audience, making it a 'show and tell' space. You're making pictures to be looked at from the front, and the silhouettes will probably reflect this. On the thrust stage you can't get away with anything, often not even wig lace. You need to be making colours and shapes that move together, swirl, interact from every vantage point. 'Behind' surprises won't work for instance!

The first glimpse of the costume sketch fills in a lot of blanks, and unless one's vision of character is totally different, the first look gives the second step towards the complete picture. Costume sketches more along the story line of the play, that combine characters, embodying one scene or another, make me feel as though my individual character has not been fully formed, nor given enough attention.

Martha Henry

COLOUR CHART FOR SCENES

Reduce in scale all costume drawings for each scene. This can be achieved through re-sketching the silhouette or by reduction through photocopying. Create a page for each scene by attaching the appropriate characters along the base edge of the larger page. Above each character, add in vertical lines to divide them from each other.

The proposed costume colour scheme can be applied to the space above each character. From this chart, the designer better observes relationships of proposed colour and texture. The colour swatch is initially applied with watercolour or gouache. Avoid using fabric swatches at this point. Mix and blend your colours to complement and contrast with one other. Observe those colours and values which stand out from others, keep them relative to their importance in the play. Note the cool and hot colours, and consider how they will work for or against the intended mood. Refine and re-balance the inter-relationships, make colour serve the scene and support character.

13 REFERENCES AND RESOURCES

This chapter is a reference section. The information should help the designer establish dates. The list of artists and playwrights is not intended to be comprehensive, merely a guide to a research, from which the reader can develop his or her own library archive. Note that dates for artists and playwrights sometimes spread across the turn of a new century. The artists are listed alphabetically and the playwrights chronologically up to the twentieth century which is listed alphabetically.

BRITISH MONARCHS FROM 1066

William I	1066–1087
William II	1087–1100
Henry I	1100–1135
Stephen	1135–1154
Henry II	1154–1189
Richard I	1189–1199
John	1199–1216
Henry III	1216–1272
Edward I	1272–1307
Edward II	1307–1327
Edward III	1327–1377
Richard II	1377–1399
Henry IV	1399–1413
Henry V	1413–1422
Henry VI	1422–1461
Edward IV	1461–1483
Edward V	1483
Richard III	1483–1485
Henry VII	1485–1509
Henry VIII	1509–1547

Queens of Henry VIII

Catherine of Aragon	1509–1533
Anne Boleyn	1533–1536
Jane Seymour	1536
Anne of Cleves	1540
Catherine Howard	1540–1542
Catherine Parr	1542–1547

Edward VI	1547–1553
Mary	1553–1558
Elizabeth I	1558–1603
James I	1603–1625
Charles I	1625–1649
(The Protectorate	1649–1660)
Charles II	1660–1685
James II	1685–1688
William and Mary	1689–1702
Anne	1702–1714
George I	1714–1727
George II	1727–1760
George III	1760–1820
(Regency	1810–1820)
George IV	1820–1830
William IV	1830–1837
Victoria	1837–1901
Edward VII	1901–1910
George V	1910–1936
Edward VIII	1936
George VI	1936–1952
Elizabeth II	1952–

FRENCH MONARCHS FROM 1031

Henri I	1031–1060
Philippe I	1060–1108

Louis VI le Gros	1108–1137
Louis VII le Jeune	1137–1180
Philippe II Auguste	1180–1223
Louis VIII	1223–1226
Louis IX ou Saint Louis	1226–1270
Philippe III le Hardi	1270–1285
Philippe IV le Bel	1285–1314
Louis X le Hutin	1314–1316
Philippe V le Long	1316–1322
Charles IV le Bel	1322–1328
Philippe VI	1328–1350
Jean II le Bon	1350–1364
Charles V	1364–1380
Charles VI	1380–1422
Charles VII	1422–1461
Louis XI	1461–1483
Charles VIII	1483–1498
Louis XII	1498–1515
Francis I	1515–1547
Henry II	1547–1559
Francis II	1559–1560
Charles IX	1560–1574
Henry III	1574–1589
Henry IV	1589–1610
Louis XIII	1610–1643
Louis XIV	1643–1715
Louis XV	1715–1774
Louis XVI	1774–1793
(Directory	1795–1799)
(Consulate	1799–1804)
(Empire – Napoleon	1804–1814)
Louis XVIII	1814–1822
Charles X	1822–1830
Louis Philippe	1830–1848

ARTISTS

15th Century

Giovanni Bellini, Boticelli, Durer, Van Eyck, Fra Giovanni da Fiesole (Fra Angelico), Piero della Francesca, Lorenzo Ghiberti, Ghirlandaio, Filippo Lippi, Mantegna, Masaccio, Hans Memling, Antonello da Messina, Paolo Uccello, Verrocchio, Leonardo da Vinci, Rogier van der Weyden.

16th Century

Simon Bennink, Hieronymus Bosch, Pieter and Jan Breughel, Bronzino, Annibale Carracci, Jean Clouet, Correggio, Durer, Hans Eworth, El Greco, Nicholas Hilliard, Hans Holbein, Lorenzo Lotto, Quetin Metsys, Michelangelo, Antonio Moro, Raphael, Andrea del Sarto, Titian, Veronese.

17th Century

Abraham Bosse, Victor Boucquet, Hendrick der Brugghen, A de Bruyn, Jacques Callot, Peter Candido, Caravaggio, Philippe de Champaigne, Sanchez Coello, Pantoja de la Cruz, Gerard Dou, Anthony van Dyck, Pierre Fierens, Leonard Gaultier, Gentileschi, Frans Hals, Gerrit van Honthorst, Pieter de Hooch, Claes Jansz, Thomas de Leu, Claude Lorrain, Nicholas de Mathoniere, Pierre Mignard, Antonio Mor, Giovanni Moroni, B E Murillo, Mathieu le Nain, Adriaen van Ostade, Francois Pourbus, Nicholas Poussin, Rembrandt, Juan Ricci, Peter Paul Rubens, Jan Sterrn, Cesare Vecellio, Diego Velasquez, Vermeer, Aeneas Vico, Visscher, Francisco de Zurbaran.

18th Century

William Blake, Boucher, Canaletto, John Constable, Giuseppe Maria Crespi, Fragonard, Johann Heinrich Fuseli, Gainsborough, Greuze, William Hogarth, Wenceslaus Hollar, Ingres, Inigo Jones, Godfrey Kneller, Lancret, Thomas Lawrence, Vigee Lebrun, Peter Lely, Pietro Longhi, Nattier, Piranesi, Henry Raeburn, Joshua Reynolds, George Romney, Rowlandson, Gionanni Battista Tiepolo, Watteau, Joseph Wright.

19th Century

Bastien-Lepage, Emile Bernard, Richard Parkes Bonington, Bonnard, Edward Burne-Jones, Paul Cezanne, Giorgio de Chirico, George Clausen, Cruikshank, Degas, Delacroix, Raoul Dufy, Stanhope Forbes, Eric Forbes-Robertson, Casper David Freidrich, William Frith, Paul Gauguin, Giacometti, Van Gogh, Spencer Gore, Goya, James Guthrie, Holman Hunt, Toulouse-

Lautrec, Leger, Edouard Manet, Matisse, George du Maurier, Phil May, John Millais, Joan Miro, Modigliani, Claude Monet, William Morris, Odilon, Redon, Renoir, Rodin, Daniel Gabriel Rossetti, J S Sargent, Seurat, Walter Sickert, James Tissot, Edouard Vuillard, James MacNeill Whistler, Franz Winterhalter.

20th Century

Michael Andrews, Francis Bacon, Balthus, Ernst Barlach, Max Beckmann, Bonnard, George Braque, Lovis Corinth, Le Courbusier, Charles Demuth, Andre Derain, Otto Dix, Ensor, Max Ernst, Lyonel Feininger, Roger de la Fresnaye, Lucien Freud, Richard Gerstl, Alberto Giacometti, Juan Gris, George Grosz, Erich Heckel, Albert Henrich, David Hockney, Edward Hopper, Carl Hubbuch, Augustus John, Gwen John, Kirchner, R B Kitaj, Paul Klee, Klimt, Oskar Kokoschka, Kaethe Kollwitz, Willem de Kooning, John Lavery, Rico Lebrun, F Leger, Richard Lindner, Henry Moore, Munch, Emile Nolde, Odilon, Jules Pascin, Picasso, John Piper, Rauschenberg, Redon, Paula Rego, Larry Rivers, Georges Roualt, Christian Schad, Egon Schiele, Rudolf Schlichter, Stanley Spencer, Graham Sutherland, Vuillard, Andrew Wyeth.

Playwrights

Athenian Playwrights

Chronologically: Aeschylus, Sophocles , Euripedes , Aristophanes, Menander .

Roman Comedy

Chronologically: Plautus, Terence.

16th Century

Chronologically: Thomas Wyatt, Edmund Spencer, Philip Sidney, John Lyly, Robert Greene, George Chapman, Daniel Samuel, Christopher Marlowe, William Shakespeare, John Fletcher, Philip Massinger, Francis Beaumont, Richard Broome, Nathaniel Field, James Shirley, Thomas Kyd, Thomas Heywood.

17th Century

Chronologically: John Dryden, John Webster, George Etheridge, William Wycherley, John Dennis, William Congreve, Colley Cibber, Ambrose Philips, Joseph Addison, Richard Steele, Nicholas Rowe, George Farquhar, John Gay, George Lillo.

18th Century

Chronologically: James Thomson, Edward Moore, David Garrick, John Home, Oliver Goldsmith, Richard Cumberland, George Colemen, Hugh Kelly, Richard Brinsley, Sheridan, Thomas Morton, W T Moncrieff.

19th Century

Chronologically: Thomas Holcroft, J R Planche, G D Pitt, J B Buckstone, Douglas Jerrold, C H Selby, G H Rodwell, Alexandre Dumas, Charles Maturin, N Gogol, J P Simpson, J M Morton, J Oxenford, T Taylor, J E Carpenter, D Bouccicault, A N Ostrovsky, J P Wooler, Alexandre Dumas (son), T W Robertson, V Sardou, W S Gilbert, S Grundy, H A Jones, A W Pinero, A Schnitzler, Ibsen, D Marshall, Oscar Wilde, W G Robertson, L Pirandello, H J Byron, C H Hazlewood, W H Abel, J Galsworthy, S Phillips, H Granville Barker, Gilbert & Sullivan (D'Oyly Carte), Georges Feydeau, Anton Chekhov, Strindberg, Hauptmann, Brandon Thomas, George Bernard Shaw.

20th Century

Edward Albe, Woody Allen, John Arden, Antonin Artaud, W H Auden & Christopher Isherwood, Alan Ayckbourn, Thomas Babe, Enid Bagnold, Harley Granville Barker, Peter Barnes, J M Barrie, Samuel Beckett, Alan Bennett, Steven Berkoff, Bridget Boland, Robert Bolt, Edward Bond, Clare Boothe, Bertolt Brecht, Howard Brenton, Neil LaBute, Chekhov, Michael Christofer, Caryl Churchill, Jean Cocteau, Pierre Corneille, Noel Coward, Shelagh Delaney, David Edgar, T S Eliot, Harvey Fierstein,

Dario Fo, Donald Freed, Brian Friel, Pam Gems, Jean Genet, Francis Goodrich & Albert Hackett, Simon Gray, Lady Gregory, John Guare, Christopher Hampton, David Hare, Ronald Harwood, David Hirson, Ron Hutchinson, David Henry Hwang, Anne Jellicoe, Tony Kushner, Mike Leigh, Doris Lessing, Frederico Garcia Lorca, David Mamet, Mark Medoff, Louis Mellis & David Scinto, Arthur Miller, Ferenc Molnar, Iris Murdoch, Edna O'Brien, Richard O'Brien, Sean O'Casey, Eugene O'Neill, Joe Orton, John Osborne, Alexander Ostrovsky, Arthur Wing Pinero, Harold Pinter, Luigi Pirandello, Piscator, Dennis Potter, J B Priestley, Terence Rattigan, Anne Ridler, Elizabeth Robbins, Edmond Rostand, Willy Russell, Dorothy Sayers, Anthony Shaffer, Peter Shaffer, Wallace Shawn, Sam Shepard, Martin Sherman, Neil Simon, Dodie Smith, Stephen Sondheim, Muriel Spark, Tom Stoppard, J M Synge, Ben Travers, Sophie Treadwell, Jane Wagner, George F Walker, Keith Waterhouse, Arnold Wesker, Tennessee Williams, Thorton Wilder, Snoo Wilson.

FASHION AND PRACTICAL DESIGN INVENTION

This list is intended to form a base to which you should add any other achievements you come across which affect period design.

Eyeglasses were worn in the beginning of the seventeenth century

1824	Mass-produced, ready-made clothing established in Paris
1859	Sewing machine
1883	Invention of synthetic fibre
1885	America discovers the game of golf (from Scotland)
1900	Portable camera available
1900	American Charles Chandler arrives in Britain with his new drink Coca Cola
1903	Safety razor
1904	Books of stamps go on sale, 24 for two shillings
1905	Aspirin goes on sale in Britain
1909	British subjects over 70 entitled to a pension
1910	Washing machine with a crank handle
1911	The Shops Act entitles all employees to a half-day holiday once a week
1913	The world's first stainless steel is cast in Sheffield
1913	The zipper
1914	The bra
1915	Photographs on British passports
1916	Tennis shoes
1917	Women permitted to drive taxis
1918	Women over 30 granted the right to vote, men can vote at 21
1920	Paper handkerchiefs
1920	Military conscription abolished
1921	Chanel No. 5
1921	Plasters
1921	Birth-control clinic opened in London by Dr Marie Stopes
1921	Postmen stop Sunday deliveries
1923	Big Ben broadcast on the wireless
1927	It's possible to telephone US from Britain
1928	Women may vote at the age of 21
1928	Air conditioning
1928	Penicillin discovered by Alexander Fleming
1930	Pringle of Scotland introduces the knitted twinset
1931	Home hair colour
1931	Electric shaver
1933	Laundry powder
1939	Nylon stockings
1941	Wrinkle-free textiles and elastic
1946	Maisie Dunn is the first Briton to wear a bikini in public
1947	School leaving age raised to 15 in GB
1949	Clothes rationing lifted in Britain
1955	The US craze for blue jeans hits Britain
1958	Last debutantes presented to the Queen.
1958	First women peers take their seats in the House of Lords
1959	Du Pont develops Lycra
1960	Pantyhose

14 DICTIONARY OF FABRICS AND TEXTILE TERMS

Abrasion resistance
The degree to which a fabric will withstand wear through rubbing, chafing and friction.

Acetate
Origins in the nineteenth century. A man-made fibre, once called cellulose acetate rayon. Like viscose rayon it is obtained from wood pulp or cotton linters, treated with acetic acid then spun. Can be coloured before spinning. Drapes well, lightweight, with a sheen. Suitable fibre for manufacturing satin and taffetas.

Acrylic
A man-made manufactured fibre from mineral sources composed of long chain synthetic polymer.

Action stretch
Fabric with stretch and recovery in warp and in filling directions.

Aerophane
Silk gauze fabric, imitation crepe weave, coloured for trim on hats and dresses when cut on the bias.

Air permeability
Porosity of fabric measured by the ease of air through it. Determines wind resistance or warmth.

Albert cloth
Double-faced construction of woollen yarns, sometimes using two colours – heavy, warm coat fabric.

Alpaca cloth
From the alpaca goat, like mohair, soft, lightweight fabric, feels like silk.

Alpaca wool
From the alpaca goat.

Angora
From angora goat, often called mohair, classified as wool. May also be from the angora rabbit.

Appliqué
Decoration or design produced separately then applied to fabric. May be embroidered, sewn, pasted or stamped on. Found on leather, lace, velvets, woven fabrics or knits.

Astrakhan cloth
Resembles the loops of the astrakhan lamb. Found in hats and trims for coats.

Astroturf
Artificial lawn or grass-like material.

Awning cloth
Heavy, firm woven cotton duck or canvas.

Printed or woven with coloured warp stripes. Can be treated for water and fire resistance.

Backed cloth

Extra warp or filling added to single textile material, the addition may be of wool, worsted, cotton or other yarns. Adds warmth and weight – ideal for vesting, worsteds, dresses, skirts and suits.

Baize

Loosely woven, flannel-like cloth, felted with a nap on both sides. Once used to cover tables. Originally brownish red, now dyed green or red.

Beaver cloth

A heavily milled, broken twill wool made of silk warp and worsted weft. Has a soft feel like beaver fur, used on hats. Cloths with less long nap are called melton, kersey and broadcloth.

Bedford cord

Strong, heavy weave with raised cording or ribs lengthwise or warpwise in the cloth, worsted cloth of pure or mixed fibre content. Used for uniforms and riding breeches,

Bengalene

A strong, lustrous warp-faced cloth of silk with a corded effect across the width. Similar rib effect to poplin. Drapes well. Used for dresses. When cut into ribbon widths it is called grosgrain.

Blanket

Wide-width woollen fabric for blankets or overcoats.

Blazer cloth

Striped flannel fabric of wool, cotton or man-made fibres, heavily milled, used for lightweight school jackets or suits.

Bleach

To remove colour through applying a chemical agent. Always read the instructions and safety notes attached to the container.

Bleeding

Where colours mingle or run together when wet dyed.

Blistercloth

Woven or knitted cloth with a look of hollow bumps or blistering.

Botany wool

Fine merino wool, soft yet firm, used for billiard cloth, fine wool suiting and worsted fabrics.

Boucle

Surface of cloth has curly loops of yarn. Used in women's suits and coats.

Broadcloth

Tightly woven, lustrous velvety-cotton cloth, smooth face, slightly felted, used for suits. Can be with mixed fibre content of wools, silks and man-made fibres.

Brocade

Rich jacquard-woven silk fabric, with floral or scroll patterns interwoven creating a raised design. Embossed appearance, often in contrasting colours with metallic threads interwoven. Light or heavy weights for dresses or furnishings.

Brocatelle

Heavyweight brocade with filling interwoven to raise up the design.

Broderie Anglaise

Cotton cloth embroidered with white thread to form holes with centres removed.

Brushed

Woven or knitted cloth with raised nap on fibres achieved with brushes, creating a fine hairy character.

Buckram

Stiffened cotton or linen, sometimes of two layers of different open weave. Used as a stiffening for hats and garment interlining.

Buckskin

Skin of male fallow deer or ram (USA).

Burlap see Hessian

Butcher's linen

Coarse homespun linen with twill weave, also available in man-made fibres. Traditionally dyed blue with fine white stripes. Used for aprons.

Calendering

A treatment for the finish on fabric where the material is passed through steam-heated rollers. Moiré, glazed, chased and watermark finishes are results of this method.

Calico

Inexpensive, plain close-weave cotton fabric. Shows flecks of darker, less finely spun cotton.

Cambric

Fine, soft, white cotton fabric with glaze, used for pocket lining, underwear, aprons, handkerchiefs and shirts.

Candlewick

A fluffy, tufted cotton, with rows of tufts creating a design. The loops of yarn are cut to produce the tufts. Used for bedspreads and bathroom mats.

Canton flannel

A heavy, warm cotton with a twilled surface. Named after Canton, China.

Canvas

Cotton or linen, with an even weave in firm weights, for tents, sails and industrial use.

Casement

Cotton or man-made fibres suitable for hanging at windows, creates privacy yet allows light through.

Cashmere

Downy hair from the undercoat of the cashmere goat of Tibet.

Chambray

Lightweight cotton of good quality, chambray gingham is striped or checked and has a corded or combed cotton yarn in the weft. Different types available today, suitable for dresses, blouses, aprons, smocks, shirts, linings and mattress coverings.

Chantilly lace

Bobbin lace with six-sided mesh outlined in heavy thread.

Checks

Stripes in the weft with cross stripes in the warp set perpendicular to one another.

Cheesecloth

Cotton fabric, plain, soft, low-count gauze – like fibre weave. Called scrim when bleached and starched.

Chenille

A fuzzy, soft yarn of wool, cotton or man-made fibres with a caterpillar-like surface. Used for scarves, shawls and embroidery.

Chiffon
Very lightweight, transparent silk, woven with twisted filaments. A diaphanous, gauze-like fabric. Now available in other fibres.

Chino
A cotton twill or blend used in men's summer trousers in the army. Also a term for a trouser.

Chintz
Plain woven cotton, decorated with elaborate designs and then glazed. Used in furnishings.

Colourfast
A fabric that will not lose its colour through washing, wear or age.

Corduroy
A popular, hardwearing cloth made of cotton, mixed fibre and silk. Similar to needle cord, partridge cord, constitution cord and thickset – each being a broader wale than the other. The warp yarn is cut to produce a fine, soft pile in wales. The backing is plain or twill.

Cotton
Soft, vegetable fibre from the cotton pod. Origins: 3000BC.

Count of cloth
A per inch measure count of fibres in weft and warp, referred to as the picks and the ends. A cloth with the same number in each is a 'square cloth'. Pick count is a term that is synonymous with texture.

Crepe
A crinkled, lightweight fabric, many fabric types available.

Crepe de Chine
Lightweight silk with a slight twist to the warp and weft filaments, more thread in the warp.

Crepe Georgette see Georgette

Damask
Jacquard-patterned fabric, with a firm weave and gloss. Like brocade, but lighter and reversible, used in upholstery and drapery. First seen in the West in the thirteenth century.

Denim
Rugged cotton, indigo-blue warp and grey or mottled white filling, left-hand twill on face. Originated in the sixteenth century.

Dog tooth see Hound's tooth

Dotted Swiss
Sheer cotton with tufts or dots of fabric.

Double knit
Knitted in double thickness, same on both sides.

Doupion (Doupioni)
Double silk thread of thick and thin quality, spun together.

Drill
Cotton with diagonal weave running to left selvage. Used in uniforms, working clothes and ticking.

Face finish
The surface treatment including such effects as brushing, sanding, teasing and glazing.

Faille
Cotton faille has a silk warp and cotton weft. Fine, slightly stiff character, lustrous with flat ribs running across the weft. Often given a moiré treatment, making it suitable for evening dresses.

Felt

A matted, compact wool, either woven or unwoven. Felted cloths are surface treated after being woven and used for making garments

Filling see Weft

Flannel

Cotton or rayon, napped or brushed to make wool-like. Used for sheets, dresses, blouses, blankets and coats.

Flax

Natural fibre linen from the flax plant, the strongest vegetable fibre, bleached from the natural grey brown to white. Used in clothing for over 7,000 years.

Fleece fabric

A woven, knitted, fabric of wool, cotton or man-made fibre with a fine, soft, dense nap. Ideal for lining and overcoats.

Fluorescent fabric

A paint effect that produces a brilliant colour by daylight and glows under ultraviolet light. An iridescent effect that appears luminous at night.

Foulard

A silk, cotton, or man-made fabric with a width of 73cm (28in), used for men's ties and scarves.

Gabardine

The name derives from a Hebrew cloak or Middle Age mantle of wool, cotton or blend. Compactly woven cloth, with a diagonal line on the face and smooth back. Made to be water-resistant or waterproof.

Georgette (Crepe Georgette)

Heavy, sheer crepe with a herd, twisted yarn in both directions of weave.

Gingham

Cotton check or block effect, made through weaving an equal number of coloured yarns at intervals both on the warp and weft. Used for dresses and blouses, table cloths, napkins and lightweight soft furnishings.

Grosgrain

Silk or rayon warp with cotton weft, heavy-ribbed fabric. Used in ribbons for binding and trimming, ceremonial cloths, neckties and dresses. Available with a moiré treatment.

Handkerchief linen see Linen cambric

Harris tweed
Trademark of virgin wools of Scotland.

Herringbone twill

A zigzag effect in the direction of the twill, resembling the backbone of a herring. True herringbone has the same number of yarns in each direction.

Hessian (Burlap)

Coarse sacking or base upholstery cloth made of jute, hemp or cotton.

Hound's tooth (Dog tooth)

Broken check effect, based on the herringbone weave, however the check is surrounded by white or another colour and the check becomes a four-pointed star. Used in worsted and woollen tailoring fabrics.

Interfacing

Woven or non-woven fabrics used as a reinforcing between outer and lining fabrics. Some are fusible.

Interlining

1. A stiff, linen canvas used for coats.
2. A light, napped cotton, wool or other fabric used to add inner weight or warmth to a garment.

Iridescent fabric

The warp and weft are arranged so to play on the effect of light on the fabric, creating a changeable colour effect.

Jaconet

A close-weave cloth, originally cotton, with a glazed face used for dresses and in children's garments.

Jacquard

The warp thread is raised through mechanical manipulation whilst being woven. Jacquard knits and fabrics may be simple or elaborate and include brocade, brocatelle and damask. Ideal for formal garments.

Jersey

Plain stitch, knitted fabric. Produced as a circular (tube) fabric, flat or warp knitted.

Jute

Coarse, brown sacking material.

Khaki

Yellow-brown dusty earth tones with a green tinge, made in cotton, worsted, linen or mixed blends of fibre. Official colour for the English Army in 1853. Now a popular material for trousers and casual leisure wear.

Lace

A plaited or braided yarn or thread producing a porous fabric.

Lame

Metallic (laminated) threads or yarns are interwoven to produce a damask, brocade or brocatelle. Brilliant colourings of silver, aluminium, gold and copper.

Latex

By-product of the rubber tree, milkweed and poppy. Chemically treated with lactic acid to produce a compressed sheet of rubber.

Lawn

Light, thin cotton, in colours or prints, can have satin stripes. Crisp, crease-resistant finish. Can be crinkled to look like plisse fabric.

Linen

Natural fibre linen from the flax plant. Absorbs moisture, a fibre with no fuzziness which does not soil easily. A natural lustre and stiffness, creases easily yet a most appealing fabric. Used in a huge range of garments and home furnishings.

Linen cambric (Handkerchief linen)

Also available in cotton, may be of sheer or coarse weave. Used for dresses.

Linings

A stable, constructed weave used as the fabric backing for garments. Often made of lighter, thinner fabric than the outer material.

Loden cloth

Woven fabric from the Tyrol in Austria and Germany. Coarse wool with natural grease remaining. Ideal for outer wear, popular in forest-green tones.

Longcloth

Fine, soft, closely woven, high-quality cotton cloth with a slight twist in the yarn. Sized and calendered to give it lustre. Heavier than lawn, often bleached white. Used for dresses, lingerie and underwear, children's wear and sheeting.

Lycra see Spandex

Madras

The oldest name in cotton – plain weave background usually white, striped, and fine checks to form a pattern.

Matelasse

A heavy, double cloth with a soft, quilted surface effect. Made on jacquard looms. Used for coverlets, quilts, bedspreads and home furnishings. A lightweight version of the fabric is used for dresses and evening wear.

Melton

Heavy, well-milled, felted, plain, smooth-faced wool cloth, or cheaper cotton and wool mix. Used in solid colours for overcoats and uniforms – the English hunting coat is from Melton Mowbray. Also within same group are kersey, beaver, boxcloth, admiralty cloth and woollen broad cloth.

Mercerize

A finishing treatment to increase the strength and lustre of cotton yarn.

Merino

Considered the highest quality, finest wool for woollen and worsted fabrics and billiard cloth. In underwear this is a cotton and wool mixed yarn.

Mohair

From the angora goat, two and a half times as strong as wool with a soft, lustrous, hairy quality. Used in dress goods, felt hats and blended with other wool yarns for suiting and coating.

Moiré watermark

A finish for cotton, silk, acetate, rayon and nylon that gives the fabric a motif effect through crushing the surface so it reflects light with bright or dim effects.

Moleskin

Heavy sateen weave with a good napped surface effect, simulating the fur of the mole or fine suede. Also a type of soft, fleecy but thick-napped cotton fabric, used as lining for warmth.

Monk's cloth

Loosely woven coarse yarn, produces a rough, bulky cloth.

Mull

A soft, plain weave cotton yarn, which may be embroidered with a design. Derives its name from muslin, imported from India as a petticoat fabric in the seventeenth century. 'Bishop's Lawn' is a type of mull.

Muslin

Cotton fabric, varying from very lightweight sheers, to heavier, more firmly woven sheeting. May also refer to a finish on print cloths to give a dull effect and feel.

Nainsook

Fine, soft, lightweight, plain woven cotton cloth, heavier and coarser than lawn. Available in solid colour, checks, or with satin woven twill stripe creating a corded effect across fabric. Good quality nainsook has a polished side. Used in lingerie, dresses and blouses.

Nap

The fibrous pile or hairy surface on fabric, which makes it soft to touch.

Net

A loose mesh fabric of rayon, nylon, cotton or silk. Available in various twisted or knot-shaped designs, with variable weights. Used in evening dress, curtains and trim.

Ninon

Smooth, transparent, lightweight voile fabric. Double or single weave yarns may be of man-made fibres and used as curtaining. In lingerie it is made with cotton, silk, acetate or rayon.

Non-woven fabric
May be bonded through resin or thermoplastic bonding.

Nun's veiling
Plain weave, soft, lightweight and flimsy yet good quality fabric of worsted, fine wool, nylon, acrylic and polyester. Slight crepe appearance. Good draping quality, wears well. Available in plain colours and black.

Nylon
A very strong synthetic fabric – abrasion resistant, waterproof, inherently elastic quality, drip-dry. Nylon stockings were developed in 1939 and became commercially available the following year, only to disappear until the end of the Second World War.

Oilcloth
Treated with linseed-oil varnish, may be with a satin-like sheen, in plain colours or printed designs. Used for outerwear, bags and luggage.

Ombre
Graduated or shaded colour effect. The gradation is from light to dark of one colour with shading of other colours.

Organdie
Thin, light, transparent cotton fabric with a crisp starched finish. Many uses including dresses, bedspreads, blouses, curtains, babywear, millinery, neckwear and artificial flowers

Organza
Very thin, stiff, plain weave silk fabric.

Osnaburg
A coarse cotton weave with waste interwoven, strong plain-woven. Used undyed as sacking and bags.

Ottoman
Silk or man-made yarn fabric, with heavy, large, rounded, corded effect produced through a worsted yarn in the weft giving it bulk. The ribs run the length of the fabric. Ottoman plush is a silk-woven, heavy rib fabric. Used in coats, dresses, trim and curtains.

Oxford cloth
A porous cotton or cotton-blend cloth, soft, lustrous finish, sturdy for shirting and dresses. May have stripes in weave. Soils easily due to the soft, bulky filling.

Panne
Satin-faced, lustrous, velvet or silk fabric. Panne velvet has a pile which is longer than velvet yet shorter than plush. The pile is flattened down under tremendous roller pressure giving it a rich lustre.

Parachute fabric
May be of silk, nylon, cotton or polyester.

Percale
1. A medium-weight, calico-like, non-lustre cotton cloth, plain weave with a smooth face. Used for dresses, blouses and aprons.
2. Sheet percale is fine, smooth, lustrous and textured. Sometimes printed.
3. A summer coat or suit fabric, may have a moiré or glazed finish.

Pile
A surface texture of yarn, cut or uncut. Examples include corduroy and velveteen where the filling has been cut to pile. Velvet is a warp-cut pile. Terry cloth is uncut cotton pile.

Pique
Medium weight or heavy quilt structured fabric, creating a finely textured embossed cord in the warp direction (USA) and across the fabric weft (UK). A versatile cloth for children's

wear and women's dress, men's formal dress shirt fronts, and sportswear.

Plisse
A permanent treatment which shrinks part of the fabric to produce a crinkled or pleated effect. Made in cotton, acetate, or rayon fabric with stripes motif. In France plisse is of small folds, pleats and tucks. The fabric should be ironed when dry.

Plush
Warp pile cloth with a cut pile. Ground yarns may be cotton with the pile being of wool, cotton, mohair, acetate, rayon or man-made fibre.

Ply
Two or more yarns twisted together.

Pointed twill
Weaves of woollen cloth, creating a zigzag effect.

Polyester
Manufactured synthetic fabric.

Pongee
Silk fabric of natural tan colour where the warp is finer that the weft, giving it a knotty, rough weave. Interwoven silk slub provides a rough texture. It dyes successfully and evenly. Ideal for blouses, dresses, summer suits and home furnishings.

Poplin
There are many different poplin fabrics made with various types of yarn. Cotton poplin is finely ribbed with mercerized yarn in the warp, and closely woven with a thicker yarn in the weft.

Pre-shrunk
Fabrics treated so shrinkage after purchase does not occur. Most natural fibre fabrics shrink when washed unless treated beforehand. Cotton is the usual pre-shrunk fabric.

Radium
A closely woven silk, with differently twisted yarns running in warp and weft. Lightweight and soft to touch, it is used in lingerie, dresses and linings.

Raglin
A loose-fitting, sleeveless overgarment, usually called a cape. With sleeves it is a comfortably tailored coat with the sleeve attached at the underarm then in two parallel seams through to the neckline.

Ratine
A rough, woven woollen cloth with finely twisted different weight yarns, creating a knotty, spongy and bulky fabric surface. May be knitted or woven, used in coats. Cotton ratine is available, is loose, plain woven, with a rough surface.

Rayon
Manufactured fibre of regenerated cellulose, dissolved by chemicals and restored to a solid through solvent evaporation.

Sateen
Usually made from cotton or a blend, mercerized threads give the cloth a lustrous, smooth face. Cotton sateen has the weft satin thread, which is a coarser thread than the warp, on the face or surface of the fabric.

Satin
Usually of silk but can be made in acetate, rayon, and man-made fibres. The face is smooth and unbroken, lustrous, either light or

heavy weight. Satin has a dense warp thread which covers the weft completely. May be backed with cotton, making it dull. 'Duchess' is the most luxurious satin.

Scottish plaid or tartan
A coarse, durable, woollen fabric with woven colour relationships particular to the clans of Scotland.

Scrim
1. Open mesh, plain weave cotton made from carded or combed yarns in variable weights. Used for bunting, buckram and curtains.
2. Cheesecloth when bleached and sized.
3. Sheer cotton cloth, lightweight, plain weave, with single-ply yarn. Available in coloured checks and stripes, suitable for curtaining.

Seersucker
Made of cotton, nylon, silk or blends of these. Lightweight with stripes running the length of the fabric in variable thicknesses, with alternating crinkled stripes. The two warps are made of one which lies flat and another which is crinkled. The chemical treatment makes this effect permanent. Plisse is a simulated seersucker. Used for summer jackets and dresses, children's wear, bedspreads and curtaining.

Selvedge
The edge of the woven material, part of the warp. Discernibly different from the material body.

Serge
Any smooth-faced cloth with a two-up and two-down twill weave, such as worsted serge of various weights and textures. Also made of cotton, acetate, rayon, silk and blends. The high twist in wool yarns and its density makes it shine with wear – holds a crease well.

Sheeting
Plain weave card or combed cloth, light through to heavy, industrial sheeting backs artificial leather and lines boots and shoes.

Silk
A natural fibre, which is produced in filament form from the silk cocoon. The silk worm spins out two filaments which are joined through a silk gum that solidifies on contact with the air.

Silk noil
A combed-out silk waste, unsuitable for smooth silk yarns, is put to effect in woven noil.

Spandex (Lycra)
Manufactured synthetic. A trademark of Du Pont.

Stretch
The elasticity or 'give' in the weave or material.

Swatch
A small sample of fabric, useful for comparison, reference and colour testing.

Swiss cotton
A fine, often sheer yet opaque fabric. A crisp, stiff cotton is called 'Dotted Swiss'.

Taffeta
First exported to Europe in the seventeenth century, this finely woven silk or synthetic fabric has a sheen on the face and smooth surface on both front and back. The weave may be of coloured threads to create a changeable face. The fine rib across the weft lends itself to be treated with moiré. Used in dresses, blouses and suits. Variations include antique, moiré, paper, and tissue taffeta.

Tattersall
A heavyweight, woven wool – similar to kersey. The lightly milled cloth is made with bold

checks in bright colours and is a popular fabric for waistcoats, suiting and overcoats.

Terry cloth (Turkish towelling)

A cotton cloth with uncut loop pile, yarn size may differ in the same material. As a towelling it has various names which indicate design differences. Terry cloth can also be woven on the jacquard loom to produce motifs. Used in dressing gowns and beachwear.

Thermoplastic

Through a process of heat applications the textile fibre becomes plastic, making it suitable for setting into pre-determined shapes.

Thread

Thread is made from yarn, which may be plied to give it strength. Three- and six-ply threads are common.

Ticking

A compact, thickly woven cotton cloth, usually with a stripe of blue or brown. Highly durable, it is used for overalls and to cover mattresses and pillows.

Tissue

Lightweight fabrics which are categorized as tissue include: batiste, chambray, crepe, faille, gingham, organdy, taffeta and voile.

Toile

Some sheer cotton and linen materials are called toile.

Tricot

1. Warp-knitted fabric with a fine thin texture. Knitted flat.
2. A French serge lining fabric.
3. Fine woven worsted made on a tricot weave which presents fine break lines in the filling direction. A chain break effect fabric, coloured, of compact texture. Good for women's tailoring.

Turkish towelling see Terry cloth

Tweed

Rough, irregular, soft and flexible, unfinished woollen fabric. Plain weave, with a one-up, one-down structure. Tweed is generally named after the area or country of origin. Ideal for use in suiting, coats, cap cloth and sportswear.

Twill weave

A diagonal line, generally 45 degrees but steeper angles are available. There are left- and right-hand twills. The left include denim, jean cloth and ticking. The right include cassimere, cavalry twill, elastic, gabardine, serge, tackle twill, tricotine and tweed.

Ultra suede

A trademark imitation suede cloth, man-made fibre.

Unbleached

The natural condition and colour of a fabric. A cream or off-white character – in the case of cotton the waste often appears as a fine texture or burr.

Union cloth

1. A cloth with warp of cotton and weft of some re-manufactured filling. There is a nap which gives it some character.
2. A wool or worsted with mixed filling or weft fibres in the cloth.

Vegetable fibres

Abaca, coir, cotton, flax/linen, hemp, jute, kapok, manila hemp, pineapple fibre, sisal, straw.

Velour

A cut-pile cloth with a raised finish. Cotton velour has a denser pile than cotton velvet, and the pile may be on both sides. Knitted velour has a fine pile surface. A felt-like, rabbit-hair velour is used in hats.

Velveteen

A cotton velvet with a short, dense pile. Mercerized thread adds to the lustrous sheen. Used in dresses, coats, suits and home furnishings.

Viyella

A twill woven cloth of 55 per cent wool and 45 per cent cotton. A fine, soft, warm cloth, popular in checks, stripes and colours. Ideal for shirts, dresses and bedclothes.

Voile

A sheer, transparent, veiling material of lightweight cotton. Found with a satin stripe, also in silk and worsted wools.

Warp

The yarns or fibres that run lengthwise. The warp is arranged on the loom which then has the weft yarn or fibre crossed through it.

Weft (Filling)

An individual yarn which interlaces with the warp yarn at right angles. Usually has less twist than the warp.

Winceyette

A cotton or linen warp, with wool in the weft. Plain woven with a soft, brushed pile on one side. Popular for bedclothes and bedding.

Wool

Fibre from the fleece of a sheep or lamb.

Worsteds

The majority of fibre in a worsted yarn is a blend of nylon and polyester. This well-twisted, smooth yarn is to be found in many of today's garments.

Yarn

The assemblage of fibres, natural or man-made, twisted together to form a long strand suitable for weaving and knitting.

BIBLIOGRAPHY

Bradshaw, P.W., *I Wish I Could Draw* (Studio, 1941)

Chaet, B., *The Art of Drawing* (Holt, Reinhart, Winston, 1970)

Hardingham, M., *Illustrated Dictionary of Fabric* (Cassell, 1978)

Harris, M., *Designing and Making Stage Costumes* (Herbert Press, 1964)

Holt, M., *Costume and Make-Up* (Phaidon, 1999)

Ingham, R. & Covey, E., *The Costume Designer's Handbook* (Heinemann, 1992)

Johnson, U.E., *20th Century Drawings, Parts I & II* (Little, Brown, 1964)

Kohler, C., *A History of Costume* (Dover, 1928)

Kybalova, L., Herbenova, O. & Lamarova, M., *The Pictorial Encyclopedia of Fashion* (Hamlyn)

Melvill, H., *Magic of Make-Up* (Barrie & Rockliff, 1965)

Murray, P. & L., *A Dictionary of Art and Artists* (Penguin, 1975)

Oxenford, L., *Playing Period Plays* (London J. Garnet Miller Ltd., A Wheaton & Co. Ltd. 1984)

Pecktal, L., *Costume Design* (Watson-Guptill, 1993)

Queen, *The Sixties in Queen* (Ebury, 1987)

Reader's Digest, *Yesterday's Britain* (Reader's Digest, 1998)

Reid, F., *Designing for the Theatre* (A & C Black, 1996)

River, D., *A Dictionary of Textile Terms* (Dan River, 1980)

Sargent, W., *The Enjoyment and Use of Colour* (Dover, 1964)

Smith, C.R., *Book of Make-Up, Masks, and Wigs* (Rodale, 1977)

Styan, J.L., *The English Stage* (CUP, 1996)

Wallace, C., *The Pocket Book of Etiquette* (Evans Brothers, 1956)

Ward, E., *A Book of Make-Up* (Samuel French, 1930)

Willett, C. & Cunnington, P., *The History of Underclothes* (Dover, 1992)

INDEX